Ecuador

Ecuador

A Travel Journal

Henri Michaux

Translated from the French and with an introduction
by Robin Magowan

TMP

THE MARLBORO PRESS/NORTHWESTERN
Northwestern University Press
Evanston, Illinois

The Marlboro Press/Northwestern
Northwestern University Press
Evanston, Illinois 60208-4210

Originally published in French under the title *Ecuador*. Copyright
© 1968 by Éditions Gallimard. First published in English in 1970
by the University of Washington Press. Northwestern University Press
edition published 2001 by arrangement with Éditions Gallimard
and Robin Magowan. All rights reserved.

Printed in the United States of America

10 9 8 7 6 5 4 3 2 1

ISBN 0-8101-6091-9

Library of Congress Cataloging-in-Publication Data

Michaux, Henri, 1899–
   [Ecuador. English]
   Ecuador : a travel journal / Henri Michaux ; translated from
the French and with an introduction by Robin Magowan.
      p. cm. — (Marlboro travel)
   ISBN 0-8101-6091-9 (pbk. : alk. paper)
   1. Ecuador—Description and travel. 2. Michaux, Henri,
1899–   —Journeys—Ecuador. I. Title. II. Series.
F3714 .M513 2001
918.6604'7—dc21
                                2001037075

TRANSLATOR'S INTRODUCTION

The eyes are Belgian—a pale steely almost arctic blue. The shoulders wide, surprisingly. Under them the walk, the open-at-the-collar bell-bottomed manner of a man who has spent most of his early life at sea; with something added—in the bald mass of pate and probing needlelike nose—that suggests less the sailor than a wise and penetrating old seagull. Such is the author of *Ecuador*, a man who at sixty-nine has done as much as anyone to create that sense of possibility in which people are now, it seems, beginning to live. Although in America Michaux is still relatively unknown, or known mainly for his books on mescaline, in Europe he is recognized and celebrated. Poet, painter, mystic, he has received France's Grand Prix National des Lettres (which he characteristically turned down), and was recently the subject of a very beautiful *hommage* put out by *L'Herne*, with pieces by Jorge-Luis Borges, Giuseppe Ungaretti, Jean Paulhan, Raymond Bellour, Artur Lundkvist, Allen Ginsberg . . .

A book is borne out by its effects on us as readers. What we want, ideally, is something that we can day by day, year by year, digest until finally we are that book and have its responses within us. Having done just that as a translator I want to talk—not about Michaux, whose greatness seems to me incontestable, but about *Ecuador*—what it has for the man looking for something to put inside himself and grow from.

Still appetites differ. One man's nourishment is not necessarily someone else's. And even the Michaux addict may prefer something more finished, less petulant, than the author of *Ecuador*. For him there is always the seraphic stylist of *Au Pays de la Magie*, or the windowsmith of *Un Barbare en Asie*, or the word magician of the early and astonishing *Qui Je Fus*. But whereas *Qui Je Fus* is an accident, something Michaux stumbled into and had the good sense to accept, *Ecuador* (1929) is a book, has in fact BOOK stamped all over it—the book of all that Michaux is through this first real work of his to become. And this, if one is looking for something to eat and has a weakness for things that come in soft white covers, is important.

A great work of art asks of you, like the statue in Rilke's poem, that you change your life. This is fine if you already do have something that can be called a life. The advantage of *Ecuador* is that it does not and cannot presuppose that much. It requires simply that you begin it. And this we may readily do, especially if what has been bothering us is the feeling of being cut off, cut off by our cars, our homes, our civilization, our miserable skin.

For it is here that *Ecuador* begins. With Michaux trainbound on his way through the Belgium of his birth, confronting the void that his life has been. And, it being *Ecuador,* Michaux is complaining :

As for yesterday's Flemish countryside! You can't look at it without questioning everything. These little squat houses which haven't dared risk an extra story in the direction of heaven, and then suddenly there flames in the air the tall cone of a church steeple, as if there were only this in man capable of going up, of taking its chances on height.

The ground note of *Ecuador* has been struck. It will be the book of a man who wishes to ascend, who has in fact picked Ecuador for the ascension possibilities that its terrain offers. Yet even there nagging goes on. Quito, Western city life, Western scholarship, Western art —the list is endless, and as Michaux draws it up, page after querulous page, we begin to sense the full extent of all that we have been shackled with, what Michaux has in the first prose entry following his arrival termed, 'THE DIMENSION CRISIS.' Yet Michaux is man enough to recognize that the deficiency—our failure to make any sort of real contact with our surrounding elements—has at its root an equal personal deficiency, what he calls in his book's central poem, 'I Was Born with a Hole.' Accepted, named, the missing center becomes not a heart, or a window (things whose function it

vi

may incidentally take over), but an entire nerve complex, and thus the source of the new in us.

Much of the originality of *Ecuador* lies in Michaux's awareness of the fact of incompleteness, his and everything else's. Other things exist to be sure, but not very many, not as many as one would suppose. As it is the traveler has to be constantly on his guard not to be taken in by the bogus magic of fogs, by horses who appear as out of a Japanese painting brandishing their three necessary legs, by women who are not women at all but simply a transfigured bit of furniture. The traveler is He Who Seeks to Attach Himself. To attach yourself—this is the great cry of *Ecuador*, there at every page, every subentry. Attach yourself, yes, but to what? Well, Michaux answers, to anything that will let you. Mountains, sea, natives, a horse, a boat, a dead monkey, you name it, Michaux or one of his observer alter egos has tried it, tried to impose himself on it, to Michauxize it. This is why the real heroes of *Ecuador* are the parasites who do succeed, the Matapalo tree and its tiny unnamed river counterpart, 'a charming tiny fish, about as big as a thread of wool—pretty, transparent, and gelatinous'; or why the book ends as it does with a portrait of a zoo visitor who has been able to make a chimpanzee utterly dependent on him.

What the nonparasite in Michaux seeks are things that will withstand him, that he cannot enter into no matter how much he may humanly wish to. An object is something out there. Something with a name, certain measurements, a geographical location. And these Michaux gives us, as matter-of-factly as possible, using anything that comes to mind : slang, scientific terminology, that tired phrase of a half-page previous—it has done once, let's see if it will serve again. The point is not to let the writer in himself take over, dominate it with his own maudlin equipment, his preconceived responses. So Michaux proceeds, never fearing to bore the reader, and with a humility that is refreshing because it admits a basic respect for experience, experience at any level, everyday, what have you. If an object appears before Michaux, what he will do is walk around it, try kicking it a few times. If it is a mountain he will climb it, burst a lung on it, do whatever is required to prove that in spite of him it exists. And having done this he will go away, satisfied. He has found something to put beside those other objects, the 'horse,' the 'sea,' the 'wind,' which (because they move and yet for all their changes of position, their deaths, their resurrections, remain themselves whole) constitute the deep mysterious forces of Michaux's poetic universe.

The peace, the happiness that Michaux seeks is one of equilibrium, of live and let live. In a world hostilely conceived this is to be arrived at only through struggle. The object is something to be encircled, attacked, done away with. But a good object is always something of a monster, and no sooner is one aspect pinpointed and dissolved than another shows itself, and this too must be got rid of. So the whole process repeats itself, poet and object contending like a pair of endlessly squabbling children, and like these coming to a *pax* which represents less victory than simple respect for one another's determination.

The style that accompanies this combat is necessarily verbal, full of half-concealed feints, quick thrusts, witty two-or-three-word parries, none of which may ever quite succeed in silencing the object, the style, in short, of an old-fashioned fencing master. The remark suggests, I think, what is *philosophe* and eighteenth century about Michaux. If he is a poet he is also an educator. For Michaux, as for the Enlightenment, travel presents itself as a form of education, a means of attaching oneself to real objects (objects that have a life, a movement in them) and at the same time detaching oneself from all that is static and unexamined in one's make-up. Yet Michaux also realizes, as the eighteenth century did not, that travel which at its best is a tonic against prejudice can also, by the same token, become a drug. Hence the current of struggle that runs through the travel journals, the traveler seeking to resist what seems to him too incidental, too consciously contrived. Intent on the typical Michaux must accept, with whatever wit necessary, everything that befalls him as being somehow relevant. To be unable to generalize is to see one's experience cheapened. It becomes too personal, too dependent on the luck of one's face and clothes. The way out is to project oneself, one's obsessions upon experience, with an awareness at the same time of all that is provisional and incomplete in what one brings to the experience.

This method which is almost a nonmethod, a kind of Socratic ignorance redefined (one is tempted to say, in view of the later *Barbare*, orientalized), can be seen from the outset of *Ecuador* in Michaux's efforts to come to terms with the great brimming spectacle of Sea. What the initial entries do is give a preliminary reckoning of the forces involved. On the one side there are the Sea and its ally Wind and its various subjects (cloud, fish, algae, and so forth), and on the other there are Michaux and his poor blind *Boskoop* with its strange patchwork of tired newspapers and colloquialisms, its apparent inability to make anything but the most superficial contact with its marine adversary. Still Michaux, hopeful man that he is, does note certain auspicious signs. A sailor takes a pot of coffee and dumps the grounds into the sea which does, actually, for a moment, turn brown. But the gesture fails, and Michaux concludes that if something is going to be done, it had better be by him, by one of his toy selves.

Finally he is ready. He pronounces his open sesame, 'Solid Ocean,' and with this word in his mouth (glued there at the top of the page) and a pair of hypothetical roller skates on his feet, like a beautiful clown he jumps overboard, into it. For a while all goes well, he is skating giddily, imagining himself not on water but on some saintly mirage of a desert, 'alone with a she-goat, or an ass and a bag of crackers on each side of his saddle. . . .' But the Michaux imagination quickly finds that such a placid state, agreeable as it is, does not suit the real nature of the sea. So, presto, storm, a wheel falls off, and there is not time enough to glue it on and climb back on the marine roller coaster which has by now itself dissolved into the repetition of a single terrible phrase, 'canyon, canyon-mountain, mountain-canyon, tick-tock . . .'

Defeated, his limited storehouse of viable sea-responses run through, Michaux can with his new-found knowledge sit back and observe the other equally comical struggle of fish and clouds, and even find an ally of a sort in the ship's electric fans and loading tackle, monsters to be cajoled, made friends of. And the section ends with Michaux having realized the wonderful human invention which is the ship and its machinery, complacently sneering at the land, at the insect tableau which the harbor with its tugboats, barges, landing mechanisms, and so forth, presents. He has arrived at the ship in himself through his ability to eliminate what is superfluous, all too easily acquired in the sea. And the core, cut through to, is also that of the writer, whose gestures, instinctive, no sooner form than disperse themselves, what Michaux has in a later passage half-ironically called, 'the faithful gong of a word.'

Ecuador presents for Michaux a quite different problem, less because of the difficulties of its topography than because it is, by virtue of that topography, paradise. Paradise is not a place where one goes around with a silly grin across one's face. No, it is more serious than that, and Michaux in any number of inserted *vers libre* poems has managed to register the sense of displacement, of bewilderment and terror that makes paradise real, because it also represents the childhood to which it corresponds, and which is in some way its goal. The urge that page after page reveals is the paradisiacal one—to ascend, to turn oneself into sky. As Michaux himself proclaims it, in a note written shortly after his arrival, 'What the body needs is a soil and nature of the same type as the sky.' His problem and the problem of the pages devoted to Ecuador is that there are things in the way, guarding the great avenues of the sky. These things are not the Indians, but the mountains, black suprahuman presences, and Michaux is, for most of his stay, bested by them. To be sure he subjects them to his usual tactics. He talks to them, cajoles them the way you cajole a horse you want to pat. He even in a sudden burst of energy and in spite of his doctors climbs all their highest peaks, one after another, and in a moment of exaltation sneers, 'This picnic site.' But the braggadocio does not hold, and Michaux knows that if he is there, poised on some un-likely summit, it is only because the mountains have for reasons of their own spared him. At any rate they do not give him the foothold on the sky that he seeks.

For this something else is required, an agent, a Pegasus. And in this respect the two poems addressed to his horse, 'Beautiful white horse . . . giant horse of the high-reaching head' and the extra-ordinary final elegy, are central. It is at the end of the latter that the recognition that will lead to his own subsequent ascension comes. He understands that his horse, 'color of wheat, whose plumes are the milk and the wind,' carried in him an aerial self; in dying it simply regained that element, reascended. Not only does it allow him to make sense of the actual visual details of the horse's death (with its clouds, its suddenly blotted out landscape), but it also prepares him for the winged achievement of the poem, 'Remembrances,' with which the Ecuador section concludes, the poem of a man-condor flying over a world of beautiful, strange, and heretofore impossible encounters.

The world has been joined, and with it a new elemental sky-self created. But having done this Michaux must move on. And the subsequent pirogue trip down the Amazon is, by comparison, a journey within—within the precincts of his own blood and through all the dangers to which blood is subject : mosquitoes, malarial fever, leprosy, gangrene, vampire bats, which are among the things that Michaux catches or sees in evidence about him. Paradise is after all a land of the dead, and the only non-Indians that Michaux encounters are ghosts done up in clerical or administrative attire, who make strange horrible noises and laugh incessantly. Floating through this in their coffinlike pirogue, Michaux and his friend keep themselves sane by swearing. When they arrive after fifteen days at Iquitos, both are fever-stricken, and Michaux has by his whimpering taken on the real dimensions of a child, naïve, sexually curious, and a bit ashamed, ashamed of himself, and the journey that his diary reveals : 'It was stronger than I—a kind of debt toward my childhood. I know me.'

The ensuing letdown is combated by a portrait (in the form of an appendix) of the man equivalent of the Andes—the Indian. What Michaux admires in him is his inner strength—a strength greater than in any people he has ever known—a total imperviousness that translates itself into his ability to spit mischievously, to live in complete smoke, to drink for five, six, or seven days running, then all of a sudden fall down, arms crossed.

I have seen a whole settlement like this—out with their arms crossed—they got my horse frightened. There were some people still reeling about in their ponchos, but this was rarer. There were also some corpses.

Of any drug they ask the same thing, and since they know how to wait it all ends by giving them the same thing. They don't give a damn about the preliminaries, they want the intoxication to engulf them and knock them out, they want to be defeated.

The recognition extended here is one we may also apply to that one-man civilization which is Michaux : modest, *disponible* in the best Gideian sense, willing to experiment on himself (which is perhaps the highest form of courage), and at the same time totally self-absorbed by the forces of a world which must, sooner or later, become also ours. And here it must be said that it is less a vision of paradise that Michaux presents (the details are in any final sense irrelevant; *Ecuador* is not addressed to our memories but to our reflexes), than a method as to how each may liberate the child, the visionary, the poet in himself. It is at this point that Michaux the *philosophe* rejoins Michaux the poet that he incidentally is : in helping extend the frontiers of art, and with them our consciousness of own latent capacities, our depths of resistance in a world where not everything has been for all time immutably fixed. By his very honesty he has created the first wholly modern travel book.

A translation—even of a book as brief as *Ecuador*—does not come about of itself. One needs help, as much of it as one can get. Both direct help in the form of time, that gift of space which is a grant, and help simply as other people's eyes giving themselves to what is so easy to misconstrue. For the first I would like to thank the National Translation Foundation and its original director, Charles Dimoff, the sponsors of this translation. For the second a bare, hopelessly inadequate list such as this will have to do : Murray Ross, my wife Micaela, Kenneth Cornell, James Merrill, Jonathan Cott; and for the typing end of it, Diane Black. In a craft, ideally anonymous, it seems just to be able to dedicate this book (whatever in it works; the bad, I insist, is my own) to them and to Henri Michaux.

R. M.

PREFACE

A man who knows neither how to travel nor how
to keep a journal has put together this travel
journal. But at the moment of signing he is suddenly
afraid. So he casts the first stone. Here.

The Author

For two years now he has had this trip planned. He had told me, 'I'll take you along.' Two years, a constipation of a kind, and now it's all for Tuesday morning. My entire day is given over to long-range planning. I feel my face questioning itself. What an effort to get me back to myself, and how 'impure' this getting back is, as when in prayer you yield to a sexual image.

3 A.M.

I have written only this bit above, and already I am killing this trip. I who thought of it as so great. No, it will provide some pages, that's all—its daily urine.

Tuesday. Aboard the North Star *on the way to Amsterdam, the city from where I am to sail tomorrow on the* Boskoop *via the Panama Canal to Guayaquil (Ecuador)*

5:30 P.M.

I must have looked like an unlucky gambler.

That glint of joy in my friend's eye! My bags were opened and not his. Going through customs is like gambling. You really want to believe in the intercession of the occult powers, telling the custom officers, 'Leave this fellow alone, he's our man.' As for me . . . What does *he,* then, think that they said? Perhaps just that they kept quiet about me.

Amsterdam, Wednesday morning

Oh! this cold, you really have to bundle up, distribute yourself in order to oppose it.

The man with the bulk of his strength lodged in either his

15

head, heart, chest, or arms is not made for this country. In the face of weather this cold I don't know how to behave. Still not homogeneous enough . . . As for yesterday's Flemish countryside! You can't look at it without questioning everything. These little squat houses which haven't dared risk an extra story in the direction of heaven, and then suddenly there flames in the air the tall cone of a church steeple, as if there were only this in man capable of going up, of taking its chances on height.

And now for some letters to I, P, H . . . Give them each a little something to chew on.

Goodnight, gentlemen, goodnight.

At sea aboard the Boskoop

Let me see, are there thirty or thirty-one days in December? And is it two or three days that we have been at sea? In the non-calendar of the sea? Poor diary. As for what has just this minute happened I am not going to say. It's the *noon* of my day, and still I am not going to say. Better for its future to be cut off right here.

4th day at sea. 4 P.M.

To be just a ship moving proud and insolent over the great watery desert . . . The wind races up against my few tufts of hair which it shakes, then races off again, while I am left on deck. Again the wind comes against my head, and again it races off, and Lord knows when it will meet up with another forehead or whose forehead this will be, or even what it is possible to say in comparison about our two foreheads. Oh, ship-pride, oh, captain-pride, passenger-pride, you who refuse to put yourselves on a plain footing with the sea . . . except of course on that day of shipwreck . . . ah, then . . . down at last the ship goes, and with it the whole complement of masts and smokestack.

'*Haben sie fosforos?*'
'*No tengo, caballero, mais moi j'ai a lighter.*'
That's shipboard language.

If 'fosforos' sticks with you it's that it's more aflame than a match, whereas a 'lighter' is precisely that metal instrument which flicks open. A European artist of some subtlety might construct himself a nice four-footed language along these lines.

Among people on board one tie : card games. Bridge, manille, poker—the one currency in our civilization that is good anywhere.

n + 2 day of sailing

Gale. The boat is really pitching.

M. very casually asks me what is the farthest distance that herring gulls can fly. Two hundred miles? The last ones were seen yesterday morning.

It occurs to me that I am no longer quite at ease myself.

2 P.M.

The motor has stopped. We are caught in the sea swells. We have been rolling from one side to another, and were in danger of capsizing. The officers were alarmed. That restored me. Nice work, Atlantic. You know how to shake things up and show your true size.

n + 3 day at sea

Each morning after breakfast a man sits down opposite me, pulls out the still folded newspapers, and skims over the news.

17

But since he is a man from Ecuador reading in Spanish, and I . . .

It is amazing how this idiot planet with that little bit of everything which it has can be so exasperating. There are some areas so utterly expurgated of any surprise that you cannot help wondering where our real place is—whether we are not the tawdry suburb of some other globe? I feel as if I've been on this Atlantic for at least a hundred years.

*

I just came back from gambling . . . how calming that is . . . Excellent for that petrification which is the writer in one.

A few minutes ago I felt huge. But to write, write. To kill, right?

*

But just where is this voyage?

*

Among our books only unselected, modern works.

This group of impressionists . . . writers of the firefly school, of the wet envelope school, of the needlework school. This style with its touch of imagery, its touch of magic, its touch of emotion, of genius, of wit, of scholarship, its touch of everything. Impossible bazaar without any bread.

And this voyage, but where the hell is this voyage?

*Friday, January 6, '28 (having
left 27-12-27)*

To think, *Boskoop*, that perhaps some twenty-five million fish have seen us glide by, have seen your idiot rudder God knows with what thoughts, have seen it, and that's only counting the adults. And there were also those algae we passed over. And we who have known nothing, seen nothing, not one, not even those.

Boskoop! big blindman crossing the Atlantic. It would be quite the same tied up in a sack.

One understands why a good number of ships end up at the bottom of the sea. It's because they deserve it.

We'll have gone four thousand miles, and we'll have seen nothing. A bit of ground swell, some good-sized billows, spray, a few whitecaps, a waterspout or two ahead, a storm even and a couple of flying fish; in a word nothing. NOTHING.

In fifty years or less all boats will be equipped with devices to put you in touch with the water milieu—which is underwater.

But these engineers, these businessmen!

What inertia, world! Lovely, lovely boats, they say. Ah, no, idiots, idiots.

A little later

If I were a hotel-keeper, my rooms underwater; what swishings down there as the pearly tails flash among the dream-rapt algae.

*

Always putting themselves above nature, never within.

If it were not for the expense they would make their cars thirty feet high and have nothing more to do with the soil, grass, and insects.

Evening

Concerning railroads consider the following innovation on the Paris-Versailles line: three-dimensional movies, kinetic sculpture. The sculptures (either wax or clay ones) would be set right in the rubbish itself. One of them every three feet. They would be seen, superimposed, one on the next, give the first sketch of a gesture, and of course be mobile. A nonstop train to be set at a previously

19

determined speed (naturally you'd have to take into account one or two irregularities). But think what a nice system for really new nightmares. Yeah! It might be possible once more actually to faint on a train.*

Solid Ocean

January 10

Ocean, what a beautiful plaything we would make of you if only your surface with that stupefying look which it has—that look of firm gelatin—were actually capable of keeping a man up.

We would go walking over you. On bad weather days we would ride at incredible speeds down over your white vertiginous slopes.

We'd go by sled, and even on foot.

He'd be quite a man who would go out alone, alone on a great wave of the Atlantic, alone with a she-goat, or an ass and a bag of crackers on each side of his saddle, or as in olden days with a caravan, a long caravan.

All of a sudden storm. Before long not an ass without one of his hoofs split, the storm has them, now down on their knees, now on the crests of the waves—there on the crests like sides of bacon (not to mention the hunting of the sea serpent, who takes off like a fart . . .).

All this aside, what a desert, what a gasp of a desert!

Immense horizon all of a sudden opened to roller skating! And imagine the poor man who in the deep by accident loses one of his wheels. And it can happen just like that, it comes off, one wave grabs it, another takes it back, and just try to run after it, hidden as it is now and you yourself sliding on only three wheels.

Unlucky the man who in a full Caribbean storm has one of his wheels break off. At the top of a wave he hurtles off course,

* The principle for this already exists in the Angkor Wat sculptures. When you go by them on a horse they seem to be dancing.

gets thrown on his ribs, only to fall, arms flailing, into the trough.

But the energy of hope-against-hope saves his bones. Ah, a minute's respite. If only there were time to adjust his spare wheel. But waves deafer than pots, waves deafer than emperors, waves deafer than mountains grab him just as he is, with his three wheels and pieces of the fourth, grab him laughing from up above, and carry him out to where they can all play catch with him and have a jolly time.

As for the man himself—like a cyclist in a canyon. Only this canyon becomes mountain and ejects him by shooting him back down to its bottom; the bottom becomes mountain, jacks him up and then blasts him overboard, the mountain becomes canyon, canyon-mountain, mountain-canyon, tick-tock, tick-tock.

His snug-fitting sweater conceals a couple of broken ribs, his back feels as if it has been staved in with a great plank. Blood is streaming out of his mouth, which is to say that it's serious, that a doctor ought to be called.

But who are the doctors signed on for the Caribbean?

The hurt man whistles into his long safety whistle, he hauls out his safety flare.

But no, nothing. He looks to see if there is not somewhere, anywhere, a light. Nothing! A person, then, somewhere. Nothing! A spy somewhere. Nothing! A noise somewhere. Nothing! Mountain-canyons, mountain-canyons, mountain-canyons. He would like to scribble a few words, an address. But he has been much too tossed around. A few more seconds and he breathes his last.

Ambulances! Ambulances!

Ambulances and nurses who always arrive too late with not a button missing. 'There's the young man, that's him just as he is.'

No, the Caribbean does not fool around. Like the Bay of Biscay—both of them rough and treacherous.

'Shall we, my children, make a pilgrimage?'

'Shall we make a pilgrimage to this Caribbean which has shaken my son to death?'

And off they go. To inquire, '. . . so this is the way you played with our brother up to his death?'

And while they thus chatted the sea all around them became mild as a light breeze.*

Big scattered clouds.

An immense island of shadow accompanies them faithfully over the water, and no doubt certain fish who enjoy both shade and only a little depth are also faithfully following these. But the pace is fast, and they have to give it all they've got with their fins. This quickly tires them. Soon a number of them, letting on that they find the water a bit cold, turn away, looking very nonchalant.

Thursday, January 12

To think that I have not yet had cause to speak of the loading booms. These masses exposed on the deck in front of me, glowing in the least bit of sunlight, giants of tremendous weight sleeping, neatly stacked, three on three, not getting up during the day nor, presumably, at night. But if it were night how funny it would be if they in their full weight, delicately, fearing lest the deck cave in, with that delicacy of the very large beast (as in the well-known case of the elephant) . . .

Were they one night very cautiously to set forth, on tiptoes across the deck; or like revolving tops with that so very stylish spin (obviously overcoming all the roll and pitch); stealthily making their way while the lookout is fast asleep.

More animated what they say than anything during the day. More hush-hush, more curl-your-tongue-seven-times-before-you-speak. Speeches and big welcomings. Each one of them with his own ceremonial manner—not something you could well miss. And they are equal. Not as brothers, or old people are. Each

* Plaything dedicated to Miss Françoise Supervielle.

knows just as many ports as the next, and the way of unloading there.

In the moonlight making their great greetings . . .

Electric fans. There are two in the lounge where I am writing. Ingratitude not to speak of them. First the one nearest me, no more than eight feet away, and taller by a good head. At the far limit of his movement looks me square in the face, on my forehead, right there on my pineal eye; rushes over, gives me a full, long look, and then jerkily starts away. With each shake of his head he shows me his contempt, more and more, then utter. Finally recoils. After a while he's once more inching his way back—as if I might after all be worth some additional inspection —and looks me straight up and down. Disdain, though, being obviously his most developed attribute, he once more turns aside and starts off, and goes away, and does this a hundred times in the time it takes me to write a couple of pages. From the other, farther off, I do not feel one molecule of the air which he is busily blowing about. His manner is that of the man who retouches, evens out his predecessor's work, meanwhile keeping his one round eye on what the other fellow is doing, and working, as he inspects, like any good inspector.

Curaçao to starboard.

From afar for hours you follow the bend of the coastline.

Then there you are suddenly headed right for the harbor entrance. There is—within a cable length—just everything, and your eyes see nothing and your brain understands nothing.

For sometime yet they remain sailors. It has all too rapidly crystallized. What joy if we had been given one lone house in the Atlantic, with a door and a lean-to, and maybe a day later a sandbox with a baby by it.

23

But no, for fifteen days I'm deprived of everything, and then in a single minute a whole town rushes up on me, thousands of houses, and warehouses, and chimneys . . . God knows what I am to make of it.

*

A Negro's head has a strange expression. Almost orangutan-like. And orangutans have rather human eyes. In a Negro the eye is that bit of water in his face.

White people's eyes look as if they house a kernel which varies more or less with individual. And this kernel does not melt under a look. It is the sign of what is concealed—the cerebral phenomenon, the reflection physiognomy cannot dissolve.

*

Ghastly your first moment in a port. It looks as if you've landed in a country of engineers. Hmm! So this is what the world is like! Must you start your life all over? You walk forward awkwardly. Hmm! Finally here are some gardens and book-stores and houses where no one is doing anything, and you breathe.

*

Our *Boskoop* at sea : dignified and reserved. But here! With it's jacked-up loading tackle, its pulley, its dirty ropes, its whole insectlike superstructure. And then that nameless horror—its intestine of a keel. Ugh! It all gets passed by crane onto some little flat boats. When there is nothing left they go away. Punks, beggars, they haven't even got a working mast!

*

Mimicry has long seemed to me one of those idiot traps. I have felt this before, and today with my virginity of sight, or rather of observation, refurbished, let me for the umpteenth time point out the mimicry of things, of those objects which are so-called inanimate. Hundreds of cases. Thus nothing, for instance, is quite so sly as an island. I can assure you that nothing on our planet is quite so much like a cloud as an island. Each time, you see, you get taken in! If only the ship captains weren't dead set against going over for a closer look . . .

Among more everyday items the Negroes' felt hats, oily and greasy as pieces of machinery—obviously trying to get themselves lost and not found again. Or Paris which, similarly, never opens itself to a stranger until the third or fourth day. Or ships, the great lot of them so grubby and rusty and disgusting that you wonder how the sea ever manages to find the rudder, let alone tell that it's a ship and not some mirage or a piece of refuse, and gets there—if indeed it does—at the end of who knows what amount of time, what blind probings, and reflections, and commentary.

Last of all this deck, as if it were of a mind to carry nothing, and be something quite different (above all, something rather insecure), this boat deck where I have spent hours this afternoon not seeing or understanding anything—mainly because of the things in crates with which it was stuffed. But What in all that was machinery and What cargo, and What just a piece of something else, or simple parasitical color?

The name. I searched for names without much success. The name: value after the fact, and then only after long familiarity.

Only painters can get much out of that first moment of contact with a strange place. Drawing, color is everything, and this suggests itself then and there. This pâté of God-knows-what, well, that's nature—but objects, no, not a one! It is only after mature, detailed inspection from different points of view that you come up with a name. A name is an object which you have detached.

To have some to detach!

The one people with no complaints about nature and its mimicry are painters (I'm speaking of those faithful copiers of external reality).

You should listen to the public in an art gallery. Suddenly a man (obviously after some moments of searching), points his finger at the painting, exclaiming, 'It's an apple tree,' and you feel him comforted.

He has detached an apple tree. There is a happy man.

*

Some locales are toxic. Either a thing speaks with us, or against us.

How do you react to a flowery red tie incessantly screaming? And there is not a man without his own wrong-way streets.

For me triply poisonous, that space around the jukebox, jammed the way it is with Ecuadorians, businessmen to the point of vomit, constantly (four times a day!) changing their suits, their shoes, their ties, and—which is the last straw—to visit a bordello they put on cream-colored gloves.

Have you noticed with what alacrity people go down to the water, or the number of paintings you have seen based on this theme? It is that it isn't ever ridiculous, it doesn't make you feel compromised, and, what's more, it isn't sectarian, it says nothing dogmatic and leaves you to think, whereas these trees, prairies, mountains . . . each of them has its one idea and says it over and over again, and you are forced to chime in.

Next day, out at sea

Just now a sailor dumped into the sea the contents of what looked like a sock, some grounds, and a little coffee.

The sea all around immediately turned brown, then . . . but what could you hope for from the Atlantic?

4:30 A.M., *January 22, after Panama*

The sea resolves all difficulties. It brings on few. It's a lot like us. It lacks the earth's hard, pulseless heart, and, be it ever so prompt to drown, we have only to take against this eventuality reasonable precautions for it to be once again our friend, quite brotherly, and understanding us perfectly.

It does not offer us these unmatched spectacles wherein the earth excels (provided we journey a few hundred miles), spectacles that make utter strangers of us, as if we were newly born and unhappy.

Who knows one sea knows the sea. Its anger, like ours. Its inner life, like ours.

What is more, it does not like the earth offer in a single vista thousands of independent, different, and personal points—trees, rocks, flowers.

To the Ancients these personal points were not negligible, and it was My Lord Rock, Madam River. The professors, after the Jews and Christians, ruined all that.

Who can now speak fittingly of a grove?

ARRIVED AT QUITO

At Quito, January 28

I salute you anyway, damnable country of Ecuador.
Still you are rather wild,
Black, black, black region of Huygra,
High, high, high province of the Chimborazo,
Strange, withdrawn, numberless inhabitants of the
                                        upper plateaus.
'Down below, look, there's Quito.'
Why, heart, why are you hitting at me so hard?
We're on our way to some friends, they're expecting us.
'Quito is behind that mountain.'
But what is there behind that mountain?
'Quito is behind that mountain.'
But what will I see behind that mountain?
And always these Indians . . .
The outskirts, the station, the municipal bank,
San Francisco Square.
How shaky it is in a car.
Now you have arrived.

*

Heavy set, brachycephalic, with tiny steps
Heavily weighted Indians careen through this city
                        wedged in a crater of the clouds.
Where is this bent procession heading?
It crosses, crisscrosses, and goes up; no more—that's
                                        the everyday life.
Quito and her mountains.
They fall on her, then in amazement recoil, as if
        holding their tongues! It's a road; you pave it.
All of us here smoke the opium of the upper altitude,
                voices low, short steps, short breath,
The dogs don't snarl much, neither do the children,
                        and not much laughter.

28

LA CORDILLERA DE LOS ANDES

The first impression is horrifying, and on the brink of
despair.
The horizon right away vanishes.
Not all the clouds are higher than us.
Infinitely, and without a break in them for as far as
you can see
These are the high plateaus of the Andes and they
stretch out, out.

Let's not be so anxious.
What we have is mountain sickness,
A few days' affair.

The soil is black and without attractions.
A soil come from within.
It has no interest in plants.
It's volcanic earth.
Naked! And the houses on top
Let it retain its nakedness;
The black nakedness of evil.

The man who doesn't like clouds
Has no business coming to Ecuador.
They're the faithful dogs of the mountain,
Huge, faithful dogs;
Loftily crowning the horizon;
The place's altitude is some ten thousand feet, so they
say,
It's hard, they say, on your heart, stomach, and
breathing,
And on every inch of the foreigner's body.

*

MIRAGE OF AN INDIAN TOWN

An extraordinary town of young girls!
There are still a few Merovingians left,
Pudgy-eyed, these people, and walking, pudgily,
Beneath the endless, enormous procession of black
clouds.
Between innocent houses and livid houses.
A slow traffic of blood clots.
And the pregnant, the police, these are the real lepers.

We were required, before entering this town, to pay
the face tax.

*

THE DIMENSION CRISIS

February 1, 1928

No, I have already said it elsewhere. This earth has had all the
exoticism washed out of it. If in a hundred years we have not
established contact with some other planet (but we will), or, next
best, with the earth's interior, humanity is finished. There is no
longer a means of living, we explode, we go to war, we perpetrate
evil of all sorts; we are, in a word, incapable of remaining any
longer on this rind. We are in mortal pain; both from the
dimensions as they now stand, and from the lack of any future
dimension to which we can turn, now that our tour of the earth
has been done to death.

(These opinions, I know, are quite sufficient to have me looked
down upon as a mind of the fourth order.)

One evil that printing has brought with it—blackness. Ah! blackness in this modern age!

Monday

I'm not that good; so I miss much of what is understandable. That's too bad.

In the carpeting of their rooms, where there are only little spots of light, a few lines, a spot, a bit of something torn, the sick see little devils.

In the same way I too have looked—not neurotically, or out of fear, but kindly rather. This, then, is one of those nothings:

Seen on a blank wall

Your silence, furniture, of wood at rest . . .
And even so you are singing
Propped as you are against this large, white, and very
            cold and terrified madman
Who is himself not yet back from some unlikely
            incident
For whom there's no more hope (I know, I'm on the
            in).
Sings, moreover, in the same way that anyone normally
            sings.
And what is this funereal gleam on your out of line
            forehead?
Oh, excuse me, lady—I hadn't seen you, on the side as
            you were, and almost in back,
Your dress rustles so naturally, quite covering all of
            you,
Which is the size of a hand, covered up to your mouth.

But what is that panic-stricken mouth of yours crying
out?
Meanwhile your hand clasps its vial, clasps it so firmly,
so well . . .
Lady, this furniture beside you knows how to sing.
It has, let me assure you, done so quite often.
It's singing—it asks only that a little attention be paid.
Stay, if you've time.
Was it to this big madman that you've been speaking,
you,
That you've been crying out?

Tuesday, mid-February

A countryside or foreign city may be set apart as much by
what it lacks as by what is uniquely its own. One explanation is
this : as you can say about a work of art, 'Oh, that's very lovely,
but it's not alive, there are too many vital details left out'; in the
same way you cannot wholeheartedly accept a new town, and if
the trip there takes too little time, nothing remains and you end
up exclaiming, 'This trip passed like a dream.' Exoticism has
played a trick on us.

Despite the three weeks or so I have been here, Quito does not
yet seem to me completely real, with that kind of naturalness and
homogeneity a city we know well has (however varied its aspects
may be to a stranger).

What I miss in a foreign scene—and I am saying foreign—is
never grandeur, but smallness.

Let's examine my impressions calmly, then, and I will tell you
what I miss in both Quito and its surrounding countryside.

I miss pushcarts, pine trees, ants. There is not one tree (aside
from the eucalyptus), not a single click of wooden wheels, no
cart of any description, or cats during the day (by the way, the
wheel was *not* invented by the Incas).

My *segundo* : any foreign countryside inevitably appears somewhat masked. The details all seem to be at work on their own

without any concern for the whole. Not odd so much as contrived. Indian women here have an amazing almost Amazon-like look. The effect comes from the shape of their unornamented felt hats, as well as a naturally far-off expression—as if they were indifferent to their own faces.

So in a day you meet thousands of Amazons. The crowd can do its utmost to mask its astonishment, nonetheless they give it a sham quality, as of something out of a nightclub.

'But still,' you will tell me, 'you have never taken a trip?'

By all means, sir, and quite a few, but my impressions stick.

One thing more. Up to quite an advanced age the Indian women here wear pigtails, and since they do not put on weight (and here I come back to my first point), the city itself looks as if it does not have mature women, housewives, matrons (no doubt, this is a matter of appearance only, but so what!).

Let's face it, old women and young girls don't make a city. There are of course some white women of apparently ripe age. But it just increases the comic effect if an Indian, to become a woman, must change her race, and then change it back again in order to become an old Indian woman. Besides, I can only think of white women here as an accident, real imported goods.

February 20

Days when I feel something bothering me I go up to the top part of town where the local people live.

Earthen houses have always appealed to me. I feel as if the people living in them were saints. Calmly they give their lesson in humility, they are neither foolish nor pretentious, and somehow they give me the feeling of being, myself, quite chic (here women all use the word 'chic' as if it were the most important of words. They have influenced me).

The dark and startlingly colored poncho is a real joy to me. What a splendid triumph over the black soil.

One false note: the word *sucre* (the dollar of this country). Soocray, soocray, as it's pronounced, can you imagine a greedier, more gluttonous word?

33

All of nature is in its outer sheen : chalk, clay, rock, foliage.

But the body's rosy whiteness!

The white man is naked because he is the only one of his type. He does not fit into the system; and placed in a painting, he sticks out and makes the painter's fortune.

What would suit the body is a nature and soil of the same type as the sky.

People speak of the naked Negro. Only the white man is naked. The Negro is no more naked than a cockroach. And once you have slept with an Indian girl you find yourself wondering whether you have seen her.

On the other hand, between two white sheets all races are naked.

Somewhat later

No country really pleases me—that's the traveler I am.

Lots of little things get put together. But big ones! I have never yet seen a well-constructed city, only rarely a hillside. Never a perfect panorama!

If only I were allowed to map out a whole county . . .

later

The sentence is the passage from one point of thought to another point of thought. This passage is achieved in a thinking sleeve.

Since the size of its writer's sleeves is unknown, he finds himself judged on his passages. Soon he has the reputation of being even more lacking, more of a fool than any of his contemporaries. You forget that he had it in his sleeve to say something quite different, even the opposite of what he has said.

I'm not in Quito any more, I'm in books.

THE CASTLE AND PARK OF PACIFICO CHIRIBOGA

Monday, 19th

I was O.K. yesterday.
So it's possible to feel full and healthy.
Who would have expected breaths this deep from such
    a narrow chest?
All right, it can happen.
In places you don't know there is thus, occasionally,
    something.
Why only yesterday I saw a park!
There was this, and that, and this like that.
There was a waterfall, and water on all levels.
There was an immense horizon making its way in
    through the window.
And Mount Cotopaxi was in it.
Some clouds making a circle looked rented for the
    afternoon.
Some big wings all of a sudden got free
And egrets are rather precious,
And a well-gotten-up peacock doesn't look all that
    stupid.
The Araucaria excelsis
And last this pervasive charm,
Into which there comes this fat, extremely courteous
    man who is my host.
So close all this to nature
So close that the wild herons let themselves be captured
Coming from afar, feeling very much at home here.

35

In the apartment, in each room, water laughing and
burbling.
The dining room—huge, formal, very commodious;

A ROYAL BED

But we left.
The car took a long time getting over the Chilio pass.
We had the night in our eyes.
The black night and dense world of stars as it exists on
the Equator.
On the other side Quito comes into view, stretched out
like a man,
And in the valley the lights watching over him quiver.

REACHED THE GUADALUPE FARM

Monday (February 21?)
At the foot of the Tunguragua volcano

It was almost nightfall when I reached this part of the world
for the first time. There were still two hours of riding ahead. I
was to be accompanied by three men on horseback. I expected us
to trot. We started, instead, down over some impossible-looking
rocks. I was soon no better off than a blind man. My horse knew
the way. The darker it got, the more cautious and hesitant his
steps. I gave him his head. He turned here, then over there, then
landed on a flat space farther down. '*Un poco romantico,*' I said
stupidly (just to be saying something in what little Spanish I
knew), pointing out to my companion an immense arch of cloud
which united Mount Tunguragua with another mountain. He
did not answer. My horse was the slowest, and I lost sight of the
others, even of Mortensen's white pony. They had to wait for me.
We passed a cadaver shouldered by four Indians, but the
night was a good deal blacker. My horse whinnied, acted edgy.
Finally he decided to catch up. Below the torrent with lots of

noise and thunder. It seemed as if we were, in fact, falling in. Wrong, only the path making a sharp veer (it was the time when half of Ecuador was being flooded). Suddenly I heard some hoof-beats in the river. They were those of the man ahead. '*Se puede pasar el rio*?' I shouted (can the stream be crossed?). No answer. And I forded the stream, which did not correspond at all to its racket. You clamber up the far bank, and there it is like lots of little strips of confetti on fire. Did I really grasp the explanation furnished me? They were insects. They would flash on, 'psss,' and vanish, gone out like intermittent flares. Nothing is left, not even the site, and you stare goggle-eyed. When occasionally the light flashed against the mountains I thought I saw a house. Finally from the horses ahead there was no more sound. Mine was over some bushes. We arrived before a solitary candle, behind which lay the masonry and windows of the *hacienda*. There were also some buildings around the sides. We were in the *patio*.

A second candle appeared, then a third, and we entered a room with an American desk in it, locked.

I wondered if there was anyone living here. An hour later dinner was served; they had four candles, and you could really see the plates.

Guadalupe.   Letter to H. Cl.

Here as everywhere 999,999 out of every 1,000,000 events goofed up—ones which I simply do not know how to take.

No, I cannot give in. I have got to go on further. I'm told it's wisest to give in. In that case no, I will not be a flea. Sometimes I read closely one or another of the great writers. There is something fleaish about them, you gather that even their contemporaries thought of them as fleas.

Once I have had time to digest a little of this Guadalupe I'll have to move on; there is still a little fleadom in me waiting.

However, I am now at my rope's end. How much longer can this chicken's carcass of mine hold out?

My room overlooks a volcano.
The window of my room overlooks a volcano.
At last a volcano.
I am two steps off from a volcano.
On our property there was a volcano.
It's my music for this evening.
And this afternoon my music went '*You are going East,*
                                                    East.'

And yesterday my music went:
Riding,
Riding,
I am going riding.
I am going horseback riding in the Andes.
I spend my time on horseback.
Few phrases. The faithful gong of a word.

Saturday morning, end of February

    A habit all my own. Here is how it works. It's when I'm stretched out and for some reason sleep doesn't come. So I just stuff myself. I give myself mentally whatever I would enjoy possessing. Starting from a set of personal and always real facts (which are themselves most plausibly arranged), I manage by and by to arrive at a point where I am crowned king of several countries, or something of the sort. As a habit it goes back to my earliest memories, and not many days pass without my giving myself this satisfaction. It is why I get out of bed so much at peace. If it should happen that I have not had time for it I am cross all day, and anyone else's words or looks are abhorrent.

Beautiful white horse (but the white of his eye is pink),
Giant horse of the high-reaching head,
How much bigger your stomach must be than mine
                              which keeps getting weaker,
Your huge heart,
Your buttock muscles which for all of one day in the
    mountains have been kicking up a row inside me.
Tall, shadowy creature, how you've shaken, rolled,
                              annihilated me!
Finally you were put back in the stable.
And I was in bed.
But your great surging gaits have been swinging with
    me all through the night (like some experiment in-
                              sanity might have put me to).
Horse at the head of battle,
Very great horse,
Haven't you on your side suspected how small my heart
                              is?
Perhaps you've heard, pounding against your robe, its
                              tiny much too rapid beats?
It's giving in, I'm telling you, big inexhaustible horse,
It's giving in, and all the same today you're going to
    be taking me back in the saddle, drunk and infirm.
I've nothing against you, no.
But it's not going to work out well for me, you beauti-
                              ful inexhaustible horse.

a little later

It is quite true that always, at any one given time, the old man
is out of date. The present is for him an exoticism.

39

I should so have wanted a father. I mean like a woman . . . whom you look for, whom you choose, and if you find her it is indeed a miracle.

In some two or three years I will be able to write a novel. I am beginning, thanks to this diary, to know what there is in a day, a week, several months.

It is horrible all the same how little there is. A lot of good *that* does.

Seeing it down here on paper is like a stop sign.

Up to now I haven't had enough sense to lie. But I am going to start lying. I believe it's good for the mind. All those around me lie very naturally (as a child I lied too; the necessity of a moment, it doesn't count).

When I think that there are two or three clucks who imagine that they have reconstructed Rimbaud's life from his correspondence.

As if letters to a sister, a mother, a dorm master, a pal, ever gave out anything.

February 28

Ecuador is made up of large mountains, many of them in the 15,000-16,000-foot class.

The earth of Ecuador is crumbly. This is why it does sometimes shake, slip, and disintegrate. *Hay tempestad, hay que tener miedo.* The approach of rain is enough to make the hair stand up on any countryman's neck, knowing as he does how rain can make a mountain split and go under. Sometimes a number of them will collapse, and if the entire season has been rainy there may be nothing of the country's profile left standing. The Andes have in a single night gone out like candles, with nothing for it but to begin life all over on a whole new set of bases. That is precisely the bewildering situation which greeted the Spaniards upon their third arrival in 1511. They disembark at a port whose name I no longer remember, and advance inland—already at sea they should have seen them, these peaks which they had marked out, and which in good weather are visible for more than sixty miles. They think they have taken the wrong turn. They descend toward what is now the province of Léon. Nothing here either—a sort of cake with nothing on its top—and remember they had instituted a colony, and built or provided models for all sorts of factories and buildings. After two more days of up and down marching they suddenly saw some pieces of embedded tile, and along with them a few cattle skeletons and some crossbows and a pavilion, all set about equally apart on the periphery of the mountain, where they formed the caricature of an enormous pot. They were horrified and went back as fast as they could to Panama, where they recounted what they'd seen and had the pleasure of seeing themselves called ignoramuses, gullibles, rookies, and idiots, what idiots.

It was after this preamble that the great 1523 series of eruptions took place.

All the volcanoes functioned, gave forth, and set Ecuador back in much the same state as before. The Spaniards returning there for the fourth time (and naturally paying not the slightest attention to the Incas who had replaced the original population) would just as soon have shot as traitors those brave compatriots of theirs who had come over in 1511 and who, to a man, believed in the work of the devil.

The Incas thought that the Guanas had made up a story for

them as a way out of their tax, and ever since they say scornfully (what is now a proverb), 'If the mountain helps out the weak, it does so unawares.'

We were driving in a car on the Rio de Bamba road. It was impossible to avoid a dog. There was a hideous yelp. I turned around, but couldn't see anything. The chauffeur was meanwhile saying something in Spanish about it to my companion.

So I asked in a worried tone, 'Has he been run over?'

Com-plete-ly comes back, articulated with a satisfaction, a triumph, and with it a look absolutely indescribable, and he laughs his Homeric laugh.

After that comes the cough, a marvelous cough, a real drum of a cough which is at once applause and thunder, which lays waste his chest and gives him the sort of working over that a cyclone might to a ship's crow's-nest.

He is Doctor Sabardandrade. He does not practice medicine. He owns haciendas. But for me he is quite simply a torrent, the sort of torrent that sweeps all along with it, which has only one direction, but that it really has!

'Oh, no, I don't care for the way the mountains look here, the Alps are much nicer . . .' That's what I tell him.

He, 'Of course, I agree with you entirely. The mountains here are magnificent, huge, spacious. Just as you've said. There is nothing like that in Europe. No, nothing at all, nothing at all like this, there . . . there.' The laugh and then the cough.

'But no,' I say to him, 'No, on the contrary, I am telling you that I don't like them. Your mountains are nothing but so many hunks of earth.'

But he, wonderfully satisfied that he and I are once more of the same mind, 'That's very true, a hunk of beasts, that's what our mountains are, and a few eucalyptus trees, a hunk of wolves and pheasants, canegues (*canejo*: rabbit), lots of beasts, insects, nonpoisonous snakes, also vegetables, you know . . .'

That's the torrent and its direction. But I enjoy turning him back around, and holding him fast to the vegetables I say to him, 'In Ecuador you don't eat vegetables, only potatoes. In an acre of land it's a miracle to find a square yard of the stuff growing,' and to make my point absolutely precise I show him in the garden a radish plant thinner than a blade of grass, not fit for anything but tears.

But the doctor coming over, 'Aren't these leaves something spectacular, look at those perfectly green leaves . . .'

A sort of nervous laugh was about to strangle me, I could feel everything going in my face and chest, my whole underside was in pain . . . it was a question of either getting him to shut up, or bursting out laughing myself.

'In Europe,' I said, to get it over with, 'we don't have any beautiful plants, that I must admit . . .'

But he is once more hurtling off. 'Yes, let's face it, for beautiful plants there are no plants more beautiful than those in France. Beautiful plants are her glory, all of us here know that, believe me, and do we ever know it; it is the most civilized of countries, the country of strawberries, of wheat, of the Norman people, the country of Napoleon . . .'

My oh my! As if a current couldn't always find a slope. And I've seen him later on utterly relaxed among people in complete disagreement. He felt perfectly harmonious, and was overjoyed to a point of perfection, being himself in a disagreement more profound with each than anyone of them with anyone else, in disagreement for miles and miles, both he and his various subjects, each a butterfly wing in its elusiveness.

His hobbyhorse was the artificial vis-à-vis the natural. When a European was introduced to him, 'Heh, these mountains here, what do you think of them? Not artificial, right? That you don't have in Europe . . .'

My friend, M., somewhat taken aback, replied, 'All the same, Mont Blanc.'

'Right you are,' the doctor broke in, 'Nothing more artificial than Mont Blanc.' That was that.

43

From Guadalupe by way of Banos and Suña in the direction of Méra, and from an altitude of 6,630 ft. to 3,280 ft., i.e., from the mountain desert to the jungle

Set out at 6 A.M.

About the third hour out it was as if I were in Japan. There was in the air at that moment a type of fog play that you associate with Japan (from what painters have described for us). Some white detaches from the sky, here and there, and descends.

Here is how the fog play works. It latches onto a tree here, a mountain there. Below in the valley another is about to make off with a brown sheep, gracefully, so that while the wool is lost the basic sheep form remains. Another, farther away, has selected three eucalyptus trees, but not for long, zap! . . . and once more they are visible, back again, that's them, the third already almost whole, and off to the right one about to be taken, another behind which has just now come back, and which you look at boggle-eyed.

The lightest bits of fog conceal a *cuadra* or a couple of sugar canes, or a young, yet white tree.

Any Japanese painting looks like a resurrection. Their fogs take us with them and in some uncanny way teach us in the process how to look, to mute our gaze, considering that neither nature's face nor that of the mineral world is as firm, as unshakable as you might suppose, but rather weak, ill fitted, and subject to as many disorders as the body of a woman—which is why you follow them with compassion.

There is also the small, clinging cloud. All day it stays in some hole, or squats in a pasture corner and there sucks on a ewe, thoroughly.

Ecuador is crossed by chocolate-colored rivers.

All day I followed the bank of one of them. These streams consume a lot of earth on their way out. And more than once they may have to descend from above.

Falling, it has the look of dust. At the bottom smoke—an asphyxiating smoke—up above boiling cocoa. It is the rio Pastaza. Its fall is the *chorrera del Aguayan*, one of the world's longest (215 feet).

We are descending toward the east, the leaves are beginning to take on size.

3 A.M., 4 A.M., 5 A.M., 6 A.M.,
7 A.M., 8 A.M., 9 A.M., 10 A.M.,
11 A.M.

on horse, not setting foot on the ground except to cross over some light bridges, pretty shaky—on horse, on horse, without anything to eat or drink. This is not the place to mention my companion, a fine man, tough, merciless, almost ferocious—and yet a good companion.

12 A.M.

We have reached Suña. It is decided to spend the night there. I'd like some food. Since yesterday I haven't had a thing. But no, they insist on my smoking a cigarette.

A woman daydreaming on her elbows, beautiful picture, all you could ask for. But if you are worn out and your back hurts, what can you do but sleep?

Impossible now—conceit.

45

are consecrated to my legs, calves, and buttocks. They unstretch slowly, you have to ease the horseback riding out of them. You have to tell them everything, help them to break down the movements of the walk.

5th hour

Finally the peons! From afar you hear them whistling, it is time to eat. It's them all right. The mules are turned loose, and some large leaves, wet and still smacking of the outdoors, are brought into the light. Inside there is always a plate, some corn, mashed potatoes, an egg, a piece of chicken wing, and pimento; altogether it is known as *tamal*.

eating

Sleep is leaning on me. I must weigh something enormous. If my horse is at all like me he must feel like an elephant.

17th hour

Gossip . . . play a hand of poker . . . Oh, sleep, spirit me away from all that, with a good shove—like someone you are going to kill.

Suña, Friday, March 2, at dawn.
I had been given the family bed

For a man who sleeps in the bed, his bed speaks and speaks aloud. And whether his wife be to the left or right of him, it still does not yield to her one inch, nor allow her to make the slightest indentation. They remain each, bed and sleeper, parallel. But should in the night these two supple bodies suddenly awake and come together, that would be really something . . . or so I like to think.

Here we all are once more, ready to go, with a long rubber poncho to cover us, and that drugged disgusted look of men who have not washed themselves since the day before yesterday.

My companion has the face of a man who has wrestled all night with the idea of murder . . . or who has given in to it.

And back you go into the jungle. This jungle is heated. Like a huge apartment. You feel distrustful, ill at ease. That's the tropical jungle.

Here there is something for me.

When earlier poets sang of the trees of the north, I thought that there was some reason for it. All those smooth, lonely, naked, family-less trees with their tall trunks and branches which offer no openings. (I am thinking specially of you, O oak trees, whom I have so often inveighed against and whom everyone tried to get me to admire, you who carry all the way to your tops the sly, quick, yet absolutely meaningless laughter of all your tiny leaves.)

This, though, is for me.

Slightly naïve and silly trees of the tropics, with all your big leaves, my trees!

The jungle is huge and bustling, tall and tragic—and very human—full of things returned, or in the process of returning, to earth. Then there are the parasites that want to get up. They choose themselves a tree, but having got a good ways up, here they are again all bleating and serpenting it back to earth.

A really crowded jungle, as rich in its dead as in its living.

The forest does not inter its corpses. When a tree dies and falls, here they are all around it, pressed close together to hold it up, and hold it up they do, night and day. The dead can go on being

47

supported this way until quite rotten. Then all a parrot need do is alight and down they topple with a horrendous din—as if still madly clinging onto life—an indescribable uprooting.

Consequently the jungle has in it as many dead as alive, which is why you make no headway without a machete. The dead ones have to be cut into sections so that you can get through. In addition there are all those parasites which, as I have said, are returning to the ground. Those about to get there must be cut down. In all directions, on top, from underneath, on the sides, the machete cuts and smashes, and whatever has been knocked down must still be chopped into several more pieces, one on the right side, the other on the left. You pass over the middle one, once it has been laid flat and made low enough to be stepped over.

The tree here is not afraid of adopting a big family, and lives in the grand manner. It is festooned with orchids, fifty or more vines trying to hug it to death. Its branches are fully occupied and sagging, lived in much as bridges once were, and from a distance have about them all the velvet and softness of caterpillars, as well as the wise, considered look which long beards give.

And last of all the Great King.

What his real name is does not much matter. Here you say *Matapalo* (killer of trees). It is useless to struggle against his size.

He is at any rate the King, the Grand King, the Innkeeper, the street-porter King, the King with all the flowers, the King who is just cluttered, swarming. And this King has a crown. Not that upside-down bowl sort of thing like so many others. No, his crown is some three or five branches, none of them the same height (but twigs and leaves take care of that). The effect is astounding, truly imperial. Sometimes the crown takes the form of a cross—a cross laid out flat—at other times explosion. But always his head defiant, and dominating.

He is extremely tall, and up to quite a great height a mere trunk. Then all of a sudden you become aware that something, you don't know what, is being sketched out—his dance of defiance. No, he is still only a single branch, but his style is already present.

The *Matapalo* is also the forest's big boa snake, its big suffocater, its big strangler, its big embracer, its big conqueror of the *Chonta*, the *Uvilla*, the Red Cedar, the *Canelos*, none of which, I beg you to believe, are among the lesser order of trees.

While still young the *Matapalo* props himself up against a tree, a rather big tree, and starts growing. Little by little he gets fat and encircles the tree; little by little he gets fat and squeezes the tree; little by little he strangles it, steps on it, kills it, Matapolizes it.

When lumberjacks come to cut it down, it isn't unusual for them to find wedged in its center the huge bole of a *Cumbi* (which is like a coconut tree), or a cedar or some other vast tree, the wood of which is something quite different from what you might expect.

Over these *Matapalos* and over the whole forest it rains, torrentially and continually, sometimes without a letup for as long as twenty days.

And none of those little butt ends of clouds such as you find up north, no clouds at all.

A gray sky—but clear gray, very alert, and in its way even luminous. But if it is going to rain, it rains. All you have to do is look at how strong and big the sugar cane grows in one of the fields here (provided you know something about its tastes—that it will sop up the least moisture), and you begin to understand how the water here must have fallen and funneled its way, flowing and gurgling, down over everything.

Monday, March 5. In a plantation of banana and coffee trees and sugar cane at Méra. In a bamboo hut

Little separates me from what is outside. I feel almost outdoors. A hailstorm of lights, a thousand knives veer toward me. The bamboo lets everything through, shouts, noises, even whisperings, and if someone approaches the partition from the other side, you are convinced that it is either to tell you a secret, or to spy on

49

you. What the bamboo does is provide a point of translation for all this surrounding movement.

Beyond this manicured bit of ex-jungle, spread-out tents and the festive tops of the Chonta palm.

Its tattered leaves—so many banners lifted from the enemy; and its body black as if just removed from the fire. What a banana tree looks like when it gets old.

a little later

For the first six months the palm heart keeps its tenderness. That's its leaf, its leaf is right there, being kept in the trunk for later on.

But Indians come, and in two or three blows have the tree there before you on the ground, with its project removed.

They cook it, they eat it, it's good.

You can even eat it raw.

Fires here are made out of red cedarwood, but the fire itself is redder still, and quite differently so.

It is this redness that you are not allowed to steal, no more here than anywhere else.

somewhat later

Artist, colleague; so what?

If I have to listen for twenty minutes to Mme de Sévigné, and all the sweet things she tells of people doing for her and that sugar-pie of a daughter . . . Yeow! That woman!

Sometimes in the evening you hear a baby crying, crying as only the children of man can . . . Ah, yes, it's your neighbor, of course. However, you inquire discreetly if there is not in the vicinity a tiger who might put a stop to it.

*

Still another letter that I find myself writing to my parents. What a need I have to boast to them. It is my revenge. So much has been predicted for their good-for-nothing. Also long sentences irresistibly start one off boasting.

'I live in a bamboo hut supported by palm tree trunks. A tiger ate a mule here the other night.'

Also yesterday on my first time in the tropical forest, some real wildlife: monkeys in the treetops, snakes, butterflies . . .

Actually I don't write my letter. I never write to them. I do not trust myself to. For should the tiger chew off one of my legs, or even if I were to come down with a good case of pleurisy, they would be right one more time.

So let us have it understood—I will not write. A photograph will be quite enough, with my horse and a couple of banana trees in the background.

RETURN TRIP TO THE GUADALUPE RANCH

Friday, March 8

On the way back we both trotted and galloped (hardly ever walked). You tire less. My right leg when we go at a walk does not say anything, but that's only because it is not in its character to. It develops a cramp, and I really suffer. What I do then is smoke a lot. It is like putting a quilt around you, for protection. And I am always afraid of a heart attack. Because I know how demoralizing pain is. While all this struggle is going on inside, I myself am being reduced to near zero. Just the same I have had a pretty nice round trip.

The wind we came back in was something monstrous. The horses were happy and swift-paced. They recognized the way, and the Patate Valley evidently stirred up in them more vivid memories than it did for me, and God only knows how they must have longed for this trip back about which they could not have been forewarned, or how they must have muddled this notion around in their heads. The wind we came back in was incredible.

At times my horse would stop, at a bend (for the view?), or on the edge of the path in front of a cactus, or by a rock, and he would seem to be reflecting, combing his memories, asking himself if this was really his country, where there was such a strong wind.

Bread, bread destined for the traveler.

Come, slightly imbued as you are with tea, let me absorb you, I will not say any more. You will find your way into the most sad and distant parts of myself, I meanwhile helping you along with my oh so numerous relays. I am counting on you. Here and there you will find whole regions of devastated flesh where tiny veins, numerous as salmon in the Alaskan streams, cry out and howl, hours at a time, make themselves hoarse howling like a dog baying at the moon. And there are others who no longer cry out, who are already dry, dry as crystals, dry enough to break and for whom it may already be too late.

Want the truth? I am a pump, and a good one. However strong, even vital an impression is, it does not stay with me long. I push it aside to make room for the one following, and forget about it, and the same is true of those in the next line, and the ones after them, etc. I am supposed to be a certain number of years old. In all of my life I have never had more than fifteen days. One second to fifteen days, that is the total of my life.

RETURN TO QUITO
(this concerns the upper plateau)

Monday, March 12

Ecuador is barren and poor.
A few mounds! and the ground the color of a blood
sore

Or black as a truffle.
The paths feather-lined and steep.
Overhead a sky of mud
Then all of a sudden in the air the purest white lily of
a tall volcano.

SERENADE SOUTH AMERICAN STYLE

Quito

Occasionally around midnight you will see twenty or so huge, nine-seater cars, full of people and noise, pull into a deserted street.

Ah-hah! A new revolution! But when the police arrive on the run papers are exhibited.

O.K., that'll do, and they stand aside.

Then the cars open and out pour bass fiddles, cellos, accordions, reed organs, a set of drums, an immense variety of round-cheeked important-looking brass, and, of course, the usual guitar squadrons. Stands are set up, music sheets distributed. And the headlights all focus on this one scene.

Everyone is staring at a window, the one there, *ve, esta*.

All of a sudden the orchestra uncorks and the whole quarter wakes up.

When any one piece is finished, another takes its place, there are three orchestras and three conductors.

Just a moment ago one of the window curtains fluttered.

Watch, it's still fluttering. A girl is there behind, the very day of her birthday, there is a girl there, but no one shall see her.

After half an hour the orchestras go away carousing.

Still remaining are the young man who is holding the serenade, a guitarist, and a singer. This one starts singing popular songs in one of those love-starved voices such as exist only in Latin America, songs so direct, what's more, that you feel anxious. The girl will not be able to stand it any longer, and since the parents talk only of breaking up the engagement, she will throw herself out of the window.

Sometimes the serenade takes place before a dark, completely boarded-up house. Nothing moves. In this case it is the walls which are beseeched. You are there on the sidewalk like those who await a miracle.

Wednesday, March 14.   In town

I am a bad reader, constantly backing away from what is in front of me, out of either hatred, refusal, or bad faith.

Recently I finished one of those scholarly pieces on the graphic arts, a study of the painter Papazoff by Zeixe Man. Reading me you cannot tell that. Still what I have below is really from him. I did not leave it a shred of one of its words or ideas. There remain only the occasional phrases themselves.

To be perfectly frank, a terrible article. Were the article any good, I would have turned every one of its ideas inside out.

If the article is bad there is nothing at all left, and this often happens.

What follows is the modified text :*

---

* The flavor of the passage lies in its puns, and for these there is no real English equivalent. *Frire le diable,* for instance, which may mean something like 'fry the devil,' is better understood as a nonsense slur of 'faire rire,' i.e., give the devil a laugh. More important is the pun on *geindre,* 'to whine,' which turns on *gendre,* 'son-in-law.' And the combination succeeds to the point where in the third paragraph it becomes a name in its own right, a vocation. [Translator's note]

Après son mariage, son instinct le fit geindre Mallarmé.

Sa pose et son goût des frictions ne facilitèrent pas son abcès.

Geindre était pour lui un homme qui n'avait pas besoin de 'self,' un roteur obscur enregistrant les actes de naissance.

Soudain il s'arrête, dressant sa hune à louer sur un clapier de grandes personnes, bafouillant le modèle avec des éclats à frire le diable.

Il pouffa ... Trop facile de faire sa pieuvre au large! ...

Questionnant les trains qui répondirent comme à un fou, son monotone l'était sans précision ni joie, tel un cratère en mal de clients.

Unintelligible, you say. Well, any piece I pick up has just this effect on me. Unintelligible. That's also why I have no memory. Who would try to keep track of the unintelligible?

*

A man of critical temperament might rashly say of Plato that he is second rate, and St. Augustine, ditto—second rate, and Shakespeare and Dante and Goethe and for that matter any writer.

There are others who envy writers. But they are even more wrong.

A writer writes because it satisfies him.

Those who don't write at all have simply not been sufficiently inspired. It may be they have been born for something greater or more beautiful. Or perhaps they would write only after having been dead, or after finding themselves back in human shape following a period of being roosters or llamas or a vulture; or in the wake of some planetary or infernal sojourn, finding themselves back home after an adventure different from and yet no less essentially great than our own.

Woe to those who let just a little satisfy them!

And I, then, who am so satisfied with Ecuador!

I know a friend or two (and certainly there will be others) who will regard me as second rate, and who for $2.50 will have the eternal proof of it right under their thumbs. For them I will be 'washed up.'

If in the past to have written out of one's imagination was second rate, what about writing about a foreign scene!

Depressed this morning, I told myself, 'No matter what, you'll still be able to paint in fresh colors what you've seen.'

But the I in that me wasn't up to it, and all that appeared on the canvas were my faithful monsters and larvae, which aren't from anywhere, have nothing to do with Ecuador, and weren't about to let themselves be set down.

Well, let's get on with it—not everything has as yet gone under.

Wednesday, 21st, morning

Similarly, those who are obvious morons, I take care not to consider them as such.

The learned, the scholars, are those who have given in, and the unlettered, the morons, those who have not.

Not only religion, but every branch of learning, is subject to Pascal's wager.

'Begin by admitting this and you'll see how simple it all is, or that at any rate you won't lose thereby. For even if it's wrong you'll have acquired information, where otherwise you would have been stymied, for lack of a connection.' But there are those who rebel, who will not have any of these a priori, these approximate theories, syllogisms, hasty conclusions drawn from similar-looking appearances, and rebelling too early cut themselves off from all further knowledge. For the scientific method is a block.

It will not do to be a moron too early.

At thirty, your studies finished, it's safe, you can once more become simple, and in this way make some discoveries.

During high school I was often aware that it was the 'moron' pupils who tumbled with the greatest sureness on the very knot of the proposed theory, on what in it was most speculative and open to question.

They questioned their teacher about it, and he explained it to them over again. They, however, remained dreamers, to the jibes and catcalls of the class leaders.

In the aftermath I have noted that the point where these theories were overturned by later scholars was exactly where some fifteen-year-old moron had put his thumb.

What the bottom of the class needs is another culture, an inspired culture.

Many of them were so formed as to have been able to understand life in a way that would have been at once the most simple and modest, yet most efficacious.

As for the Catholic faith, when I studied it I really did not think very much of the bishops and fathers who gave the theology and philosophy courses. I found them a little too tricksy. Much more to my taste was the priest of Ars, blackballed from every exam and theological dispute, or Saint Joseph di Cupertino, surnamed the ass, and the admirable Ruysbrock who did everything inside out and who, while failing to grasp any number of facts did get the essential nub—*the God whom there was to love.*

Si quis videtur entre [*inter*] *vos sapiens esse in hoc saeculo, stultus fiat ut sit sapiens* (St. Paul).

It is almost an intellectual tradition to pay heed to the insane. In my case those that I most respect are the morons.

Wednesday, 21st, morning

In a few hundred years, I trust, the world will have breadth. At last! People will communicate with the animals, even speak with them. How short-sighted are those who do not see this general movement, or the meaning of various paraphysic and scientific advances in this direction.

The question then will be how such a monstrous gap in our civilization can have gone on for so long.

They will look through tears such as only the innocent can shed at our literary masterpieces, present and past. And with some admiration, too, the admiration you have for painters who have had their arms amputated and who still manage to paint with their feet. 'What!' they will say, 'With nothing but men and women to talk about they still wrote abundantly, and even not too badly.'

Ah! Woman! Friends! At last we will be able to love something else.

How confining the phrase, *Love your neighbors as yourself*, if it holds only for human beings. How good it will be, and how dearly I wish I could know what it is like to speak to a dog, to be able to ask him his thoughts and impressions. And even should he talk about his intestinal product, it would still be worth hearing. Naturally the newspaper reporters and snobs and parlor ladies of that time will exclaim, 'How very poetic.' Anyway it will all come about when I am no longer around.

How lovely the centuries ahead are going to be.

If you only knew how I would have liked to live among you.

Do not think me quite as opinionated as I may seem. I would understand, I promise you that; it's just that I am in a real hurry, under constant pressure both from what is without and from that great space of the future. But I would try.

If some man of that era can get in touch with what will be left of me, let him make the attempt, there may still be something to work with. Try!

Do not leave me for dead just because the newspapers have announced me as being no more.

I will be even humbler than I am now. I shall have to be. I am counting on you, oh future reader. Do not leave me all alone with the dead, like a soldier at the front who gets no mail. Choose me from among them if only for my great desire and concern. Speak to me, then, please, I am counting on you.

People often ask why the young of this generation are in despair. One reason is that they realize they are being sacrificed. They envisage the golden time. But they will not live in it. Would any of them not accept having his life stop in order to live in the year 2500?

This state of mind is new in the world. People expect more from the future than before.

58

You can love a woman. To admire her is hard. You are not dealing with something important.

As for man, he is a spoiled animal. Original, but never harmonious. His manner is always that of the specialist.

There are moments, however, when I think of Julius Caesar's lover.*

That was no slouch of a man. To raise his life he did what he could. The relationship with a man like Julius Caesar, engineer, mechanical whiz, field marshal, conquering explorer, who got all the way into the northernmost part of Gaul, tough with all that, and manly, always walking bare-headed, and magnanimous, how he could and must have loved him!

What an atmosphere he must have spent his days in, and what boudoir could have given as much!

But there you are—what did Julius Caesar think of his friend? That didn't do very much to raise him.

How few are the possibilities open to a man. The gift of love is wonderful, but how monotonous and lacking in surprise is its object.

I often watch dogs. Less out of vice than because I need something to think about. But those going by look at me with a smile, it gets in the way of my thoughts, and I have to go on walking.

The dog has a place quite apart in the order of mammals. Bitches furnish him with a world which in the whole of his life he will never manage to understand.

He takes on every size and shape, some of them fifteen or

* Frankly I do not any longer recall if such were in fact Caesar's predilections.

twenty times bigger than he! Here is a giantess. He does not lose heart. He has an erotic imagination, and it carries him through every scaling, each act of penetration. He will even take on dwarfs, and ones that look like babies.

He also gets completely wrapped up in what he is doing. And should an old prude come along and break her umbrella on the exhibitionist's back he will not relinquish his idea, which is profound and in its implications large.

Wednesday morning, March 21

A mind of a certain size can feel only exasperation toward a city. Nothing can drive it more fully to despair. The walls first of all, and even then all the rest is only so many horrid images of selfishness, mistrust, stupidity, and narrow-mindedness.

No need to memorize the Napoleonic code. Just look at a city and you have it.

Each time I come back from the country, just as I am starting to congratulate myself on my calmness, there breaks out a furor, a rage . . .

And I come upon my mark, *homo sapiens*, the acquisitive wolf.

Cities, architectures, how I loathe you!

Great surfaces of vaults, vaults cemented into the earth, vaults set out in compartments, forming vaults to eat in, vaults for sex, vaults on the watch, ready to open fire. How sad, sad . . .

March 29, '28

Paul Valéry has beautifully defined modern, i.e., European, civilization. But I had had my fill of it long before coming upon his point-by-point documentation of its various limits.

All I ever felt were its *lacunae*, those areas where it didn't exist. Maybe that's why during most of my childhood I seemed so inept at school work.

Oh, yes—European civilization. Well, Mr. Valéry, neither your Greeks, Romans, nor Christians have enough oxygen in them for anyone any more.

The twentieth century, they will say in the year 2500, thought the earth was flat.

There is efficacious belief—and there is theory.

The Earth isn't round—not yet—it has to be made round.

Mr. Writer says he represents the Universe. That's the new style.

Occasionally one of them may even start on a trip. He gets as far as Hong Kong and goes to bed with a Yellow Woman. He then comes home, people look at him, invite him to speak to them . . . He knows China.

The same was true of the Chinese sailors from the boat moored next to mine at Rotterdam whom I used to listen to talk about France. The abbey of Thélème, the Casino de Paris. They are still with me. I listened to them straight-faced.

March 30, '28

Last night I took some ether. What visions! What immensity!

The ether comes in a flash. As it approaches it makes the taker feel both enlarged and disproportioned—that taker being me—and prolongs him in Space, prolonging him there without avarice, with no comparison whatever. The ether arrives with the speed of an express train, over its route of leaps and straddlings. Staircase where the steps are all cliff.

In much the same way one of those great sailing Andean condors floats up through floor after floor of the atmosphere.

However my feet and legs withdraw (as if my whole material weight had been deposited on them, drop by drop), and I feel as if my extremities were made out of rubber.

And over my mouth a mouth of ice.

For young people cities are a good exercise in hatred.

But Quito! suffocation itself.

The terrestrial globe raised a shoulder there. To an altitude of 10,300 feet it succeeded in thrusting, no, not a mountain, but a valley. At 10,300 feet!

In this valley: Quito.

This mountain- and volcano-surrounded valley was not to have been this narrow.

But it was sealed up.

The Incas (for either military or religious reasons, or something equally obscure) created an artificial mountain,* the *Panecillo*, and it is this *Panecillo* which hermetically seals up the valley and blocks out the horizon.

But at least, you will say, there *are* streets . . .

But at the end there is always the *Panecillo*. The stiffneck's *Panecillo*.

But at least, you will say, then the streets themselves.

Well, that is just the point, Quito does not have streets, it has drawing rooms, and it's there, indoors, that you greet each other, '*Senorita, hijito; mi queridisimo, Buenas tardes, Buenas dias, mucho gusto de* . . .' You are everlastingly greeting one another, with no hope of ever getting it over with. And the way the system works here is that you embrace, each throws himself in the other's arms, the two of you overturning like a pair of badly managed casks. And from him you fall to the next. The girls sniff you out, from even a thousand yards off, and I hate them all and walk stiff and straight and quickly and blind as a machine, and feeling poisoned as can be.

What's more, this city has no running water.

---

* The explanation is fanciful. But it is one current here.

The house of my hosts is undergoing alterations. They consulted me, I had some ideas, I was quite happy about it, I like working with my hands, creating things. Plans for patios, rooms, pieces of furniture. Knocking down things, altering them, destroying them, redoing them, changing them around. There were walls to be laid out in Hispano-Mauresque style, fountain places, walnut and cedar trees, decorative tiles, mosaics, cow bones.

I do it with my friend. His room is finished.

So today he says, pointing out a little farther on, 'That's to be your room . . . You see, right there, with a patio on each side, lots of light . . .'

My room! My room!

It is amazing how you can be perspiring heavily and at the next moment feel quite cold. This change of speed has not been well studied up to now. My room! What a mess! Have me construct my own room! Ugh! You can put me anywhere—on the ground. My room. So they want me to spend all the rest of my days in Quito!

Money, money, one of these days I will say something about you. There is not in this century one poet who will not attribute his actions to the pressure of money. As far back as you want, my life has been in this straitjacket.

But let us be calm. Perhaps it is just the effect of combining laudanum with ether. Perhaps the resulting sensation on my forehead of a circle of fire simply depicted a little too vividly what he was telling me, words which I accidentally interpreted as my condemnation. No, these people here are not Europeans.

The American builds a palace. This lasts a while, and then he finds a doorman and gives him the keys and goes away, and that is all there is to it.

But my friend has a library in which he has been putting aside books for himself and for me.

And that is serious, very serious. He asks me which of them I want. I answer—none.

He does not understand and has brought up those which I ought to like.

In all truth he is my very perplexed and very close friend.

But I to him!

Can you have a traitor as a friend!

That is not my key, Traitor. It is yours now.

When in the course of a winter night in Quito the ether addict (his doors, of course, barred) hears across his milky fog the scream of police whistles . . .

(And keep this in mind for later use: Quito's police force, unmatched both in sheer manpower and in the frequency with which its calls crisscross back and forth at night across the city.)

All of a sudden one winter night the Quito ether addict hears a cold whistle. Is someone coming? What? that occasions such a poignant, such a tragic sound.

Some time goes by, then more time, an immense cascade of time.

Infinitude.

But look, it is as if someone were trying to tear my shirt off.

'*Quiere un poco mas?*'

In front of me is the man with the flask of ether, who pours me some. Well, Infinity, so that is all it was! Well! The fog has, meanwhile, been giving me time to recover.

Infinity . . . infinity all the same.

Infinite mistake of the man who would think that . . . because, it is only, that I . . .

The speed . . .

The sense of being far away . . .

The water . . .

As a region Ecuador is set apart both by its altitude, which ranges from zero to 19,000 feet at its center, and by its place on the globe, which its name already indicates.

The highest part is snow and ice, the skullcap of hundreds of volcanoes. The middle region (around 10,000 feet) is still cold and arid. Half an hour in a slow train and you arrive at a station, they offer you freshly picked tangerines. You are stung by gnats. You cannot stand an overcoat any more (it is that you have got down to 7,500 feet). Still a few minutes to go : sugar cane, and then a few hundred feet farther on, i.e., around 3,300 feet, and there are pineapples, banana trees, palm trees of all types, monkeys, parrots, signs of typhoid and malaria.

The middle region is both the most civilized and most populated, containing the capital and most of the cities. It is a patch of earth about as big as Serbia, the rest being the size of France.

(The governments of Ecuador, Colombia, and Peru cannot get together. Their respective calculations disagree by as much as 60,000 miles.)

A plateau Ecuadorian has a Montenegrin feeling about his land. To him there is just this one patch of earth. The rest is mystery and danger.

El Oriente, an Ecuadorian says this word as if it were *Paris*, both dangerous, hard to reach, and presumably awe-inspiring.

Lots of Ecuadorians have never been east. By any yardstick it is the country's richest section. But you know what stay-at-homes workers are, no matter what their country. Besides, Ecuador is an agricultural country.

Reactionary, stubborn, not daring. Probably the least American of the Americas, the most European, modest, reserved, giving you more an impression of fussiness and lack of youth.

*

65

The climate of Ecuador is hard to specify. In the upper plateau country the people have a saying, and it's close to the truth—the four seasons in one day:

Morning summer.

Noon springtime. The sky is beginning to get overcast.

4 P.M. rain. Freshness.

A night cold and luminous like winter.

For this reason clothing is a problem if you must be out for more than a few hours.

You watch the accursed setting forth, armed with straw hat, canvas, furpiece, and umbrella.

Monday, April 4

Today departure for Puembo, once more to set out across a strip of this country of Ecuador, a country which has nothing in it but canyons. You lean out over huge crevices. What water is that gurgling down below! What? You lean out still farther. It is only some rooster piss which is flowing. The ground is so crumbly that if at the top of a mountain you overturn the contents of a small pitcher it will cut off at least three feet. Sometimes you come across a huge precipice, with a bit of dirt on top of it and people's houses. In Quito there are two such long *quebradas*, each of which has some twenty feet of superficial earth and one hundred feet of precipice. When it rains they stop the trolley cars and everyone gets out to watch the earth buckle. It may hold out a while longer.

Sometimes in a street you can hear a far off and yet very distinct sound of rushing water. At first you don't see a thing. You are by a small hole. Automatically you pick up a pebble and drop it in. To hear the noise takes so many seconds that it is all you can do not to go away. You feel yourself grabbed from down under, there is a loud throb to your steps, and in a stupid, flat voice you find yourself muttering, 'The cow floor . . . the cow floor . . .'

66

Ecuador is straight and steep.

The one time when there is shadow—and when Ecuador loses its hardness—is 5 or 6 A.M., when the sun is still down on the horizon.

The darkness, then, as at home, tucks itself away in the canyons, the mountain gives its softness to the plateau, and the men who are out walking seem to be dragging behind the most indolent part of themselves. Even the donkey carts take on a distracted, stooped, muted aspect. It is the Shadow, the Shadow.

But that's soon finished, the sun gets higher, in no time it is overhead and going for one shadow after another. Soon all that is left is what you have under your feet. You are back once more under the Equator's implacable justice.

Puembo, hacienda of San José

Some pretty growths, not entirely erased. The vestiges of a very lovely park.

I like it and it enters me.

My friend, however, who has seen it all, has his plans which he announces to me, thus cutting me off from these gardens where I had found something all my own.

What birds! And with songs unknown to me. From the insistent little chirps that they pour out you would think them delighted to see us. My friend, however, who has seen it all, picks up a tube with a clay pellet, and stuns a South American sparrow. It is gathered up, put in a box, only the peasant watching failed to take care and let it fly away.

Everything here grows pell-mell. You cannot even recover the goddamn things. Then food, then it rains, then sleep, sleep, then —it must be the pastime here—out they are blowing into their tubes, the shot goes terribly far. This afternoon they killed two hummingbirds.

DEATH OF A BIRD

It was a splendid color—a *carpintero*.

I fired my charge.

It seemed to hesitate, then fell over onto a huge palm leaf.

I took it in the palm of my hand. It looked like this—gold, black, and red.

I felt it, and folded back its wings. For quite some time I examined it. *It was intact.*

It must have died of shock.

Puembo, Monday, April 5

Your face breaks out, you have a headache, your heart thumps the way it does when you have a fever. You feel completely limp, ready to break in two, wondering if you still have a ligament left capable of keeping the two ends of you together. You conjure up a serious case of food poisoning. You pass a wretched night. Next day you announce you will not eat a thing, putting the blame on the *tortilla*, or one of those innumerable stews that are Ecuador's specialty. People look at you, then say, 'Oh, no, those are mosquitos.'

'What mosquitos? There aren't any around.'

You are taken outside. You do not see anything.

'There's one.'

'But I don't see a thing.'

'Look out. You've been stung, they're all over you.'

You look at your hand, incredulous. Of course. You hadn't felt a thing.

The mosquito here with wings and feet stretched out does not in all measure one millimeter.

In spite of the most painstaking precautions you don't ever manage to feel the stings which in a few minutes completely disfigure you.

I WAS BORN WITH A HOLE

A terrible wind is blowing.
It's only a small hole in my chest,
But a hideous wind is blowing in.
Little village of Quito, you're not for me.
I need hatred, and envy, that's my meat.
A great city is what I need.
A great consummation of envy.

It's only a small hole in my chest
But a terrible wind is blowing in,
In the hole there's hatred (always), also terror and
                                        helplessness,
There's helplessness, and the wind reeks of it,
Strong as a whirlwind,
Enough to snap a steel needle,
And it's a mere wind, a void.
Fie on all the earth, on all civilization, on all the beings
    on the surfaces of all the planets, because of this
                                        void!
That critic fellow said I had no hatred.
This void, there's my answer.
Oh! are things bad under my skin!
I need to weep over the bread of luxury, and domi-
    nion, and love, over the bread of glory which is
                                        without,
I need to gaze out the windowpane,
Which is blank like me, and takes in nothing whatso-
                                        ever.
I said weep: no, it is a cold drill, drilling, tirelessly
                                        drilling
As on a rafter of beechwood where 200 generations of
    worms have bequeathed this heritage, 'drill . . .
                                        drill.'
It is on the left, but I am not saying it is my heart.

69

I said hole, I am saying no more, it is a violent pain
and I am helpless.
I have seven or eight senses. One of them : an absence.
I touch it and pat it as you would pat wood.
But, more likely, it would be a vast forest, one such as
Europe hasn't seen for ages.
And it is my life, my life in the void.
If it disappears, this void, I search myself, I get into a
frenzy and it's even worse.
I have erected myself on a missing column.
What would Christ have said had he been so con-
stituted?
There are some ailments that, cured, leave you with
nothing.
You soon die, you were too late.
Can a woman be satisfied with hatred?
Then love me, love me very much and tell it to me,
Write to me, some one of you.
But what's this little person?
I wasn't aware of him a while back.
Neither a pair of thighs, nor a great heart can fill my
void,
Nor eyes full of England and longing as the phrase
goes,
Nor a voice singing, bespeaking completion and
warmth.

My shivers have their own supply of cold.
My void is a great guzzler, a great crusher, a great
exterminator.
My void is quilting and silence.
Silence that stops everything.
A silence of stars.
Though this hole may be deep, it has no form.
Words don't find it,
Only wobble around.

I have always wondered how people who regard them-
        selves as revolutionaries should feel brotherly.
They spoke of one another with emotion: flowed like
                                                soup.
That's not hatred, my friends, that's gelatin.
Hatred is always hard,
Strikes others
But likewise perpetually scrapes its own man on his
                                                inside.
It is the opposite of hatred.
And no remedy. No remedy whatever.

NAUSEA, OR IS DEATH COMING ON?

April 27

Give up, my heart,
We've struggle enough.
And let my life stop,
One hasn't been a coward
One has done what one could.

Oh! my soul,
You're coming or going
You've got to make up your mind
Just don't prod my inner organs so
Now attentively, now absent-mindedly,
You're coming or going,
You've got to make up your mind.

For myself, I can't hold out much longer.

Lords of Death
I've neither reviled nor applauded you.
Have pity on me, veteran already of so many trips
                                without a suitcase,

Without a master either, without wealth, and the
                              glory went elsewhere,
You are powerful assuredly and above all else comical,
Have pity, therefore, on this crazed man who even be-
    fore crossing the barrier cries out to you his name,
Take him on the wing,
And then, if he suits your temperament and style, and
                              if it's possible,
And if you feel like helping him, help him, I beseech
                              you.

May 1

A letter this morning. Someone writes, 'You'll miss Ecuador
and its Indians! I have seen some (in wax) in the Berlin Museum.
What poetry is theirs!'

I had said before that I detested Indians. No, I shall have to
act the intelligent traveler, lover of the exotic. 'I have a fortune
there!' But I am saying I detest the Indians. A citizen of the
earth. Citizen! And the Earth! 'Indian,' 'Indian,' you can be
driven crazy with a word like that. An Indian is a man, yes? A
man like any other, cautious, unable to leave and getting no-
where and not even trying to, a man 'just so' (as for my getting
used to them, I have just now come down with a case of jaundice).
These people do not have saints, and besides how the hell am I
to get along with a bunch of brachycephalics?

Once for all this is it: anyone who does not contribute to my
betterment—zero.

May 2. Sickness (yellow fever)

If a man starts coming up all over the place with words like
'disgusting, nauseating, that's revolting . . .' look out. If he is a
novelist and one day has his characters without any advance
warning on their part start vomiting, ditto.

At first they told me my aorta was weak, which may well be the case. It was a question of explaining the nausea I kept feeling as if all around me was breaking down. Now I have a real case of yellow fever.

*

The obsession with vomit.

I was in Puembo ten days ago. There was a dog there with a real odor. The dog himself, by the way, was big, courteous, and faithful, with long snow-white hairs. He would walk behind me, like a major-domo, never in front. He was in fact extremely handsome, and carried himself with an elegance in both park and paramo, and had soft eyes.

O.K., now for that dog's odor. The odor of that dog was, 'Sh——! utter filth. I smear you in goose grease. After that I turn you upside down in a bed full of old, unsavory slobber and tripe, and don't you dare make a fuss. We're after all . . .' All this and a good deal more was what one spurt of this odor conveyed. I stared at that dog. I shot out my foot after him. I'd have killed him. Eventually he moved off, taking with him his cloud of slimy thoughts.

Even there his eyes remained faithful. I took some deep breaths. Then, little by little, he began coming over, all the while without knowing it shedding that carrion bag of his over my head. 'Ah, *carajo*, beat it, away with you,' and he would leave and go lie down some distance away. And sometimes, even though he was at a distance which up to then had been all right, the wind would shift, or there would be a sudden current of air . . . ah! that odor, what a lavatory!

But the dog was asleep. At such a moment I did not dare go over and hit him, or make a cough to wake him up so I could then hit him. No, he had *me* on the run. It took a while to find my way back into open country.

Chastity has on me the effect of a drug. Its symptoms : quick gestures, hostility, fear, a need for music. When I am slow I feel like a painter, stupid, accepting, and completely given over—my downfall after the woman's. *Tum viderunt quia nudi erant.*

When I am chaste no word can keep up with me. My ideas come to me with the speed needed to seize a man drowning. If in these moments I write, useless, it is never more than a résumé. Still, alas, it is my lucid optimum.

Quito, May 23

Operetta season given by a Spanish troupe.

Changed town. Performers about in the street with that prostitute's look, that look which tempts fate, which believes in possibilities, in all reconciliations, which at any rate believes and encourages us to believe that not everything in Quito has been for all time irrevocably determined.

May 10

Round word covering nearly my whole idea of Asia, and which my youth endowed with a real nostalgia—*Opium.* I know you now . . . and you're not one of mine.

This perfection without strain means nothing to me. Better ether, which is more Christian. Blasts you away from yourself.

The opium lingers in my veins. It puts calmness there, and satisfaction.

Fine. But what has that to do with me? It just embarrasses me.

And with my nerves gone, what have I got left?

May 18

Horses able to practice magic.

No, this failing common to all quadrupeds is the one really serious argument against animal intelligence (the ability to hypnotize, noticeable among certain of them, is the bare ABC).

Yesterday during cocktails at the Savoy I ran into a man to whom I had been introduced some three months ago (having, of course, forgotten both him and his name).

He took me by the arm, 'Come with me, this family doesn't suit you. What you need are the open spaces, excitement, women. I know you, come on.'

All the while shoving me downstairs, and hastily presenting me to clusters of women . . . '*Aqui, el Señor M., famoso escritor frances* . . .' and at the same whispering in my ear, 'Nice woman, that one, you know, real nice, makes love real nice'; and finally in spite of my various attempts to affirm my morality gets me into his car.

He was going on, 'You can have my horse, and we'll go to my hacienda in the *paramo. Tu quedaras* (you'll stay) *tres meses.*'

I inquired, 'The *paramo* by Mount Cotopaxi (it's the nearest)?'

'No, much higher than Mount Cotopaxi,' he answered on the spot, 'it'll make you strong, you can gallop . . .'

I asked him his name. 'Alberto,' he said. It sounded like a first name.

And the last name? 'Larrea.' Ah, *loco* (madman) Larrea.

In town it is his one name, the most popular around, earned through his superb bravery, his willingness to go all out with anything—drinking, bullfighting, driving a racing car.

'You've got to see my car.'

It is a racing Peerless. In the middle of town he corners at full speed. Not one where he does not skid three or four yards and bounce up over the curb.

At a balcony a young woman appears, very alarmed. 'You're going to be killed.'

He quickly tosses her a rendezvous. Off we go even faster.

After the bullfight there are five of us in the car. Two of them packed into the back with the tools. In the front the *loco* and I; on my right an unknown.

We start off. I tell him to step on it. In the back they are

75

whimpering, 'Not so fast!' We never slow down for a curve. The man on my right is trying to pull out the hand brake. I do all I can to prevent him. He says to me, 'It's obvious you don't know Loco Larrea. He's a madman. You don't know what he's capable of, if given a chance.'

My answer is a lunge.

We bounce from one side of the road to the other, like a sled whose dogs are badly spaced. Taking a blind corner is like going into the void. I say, 'Great . . . great . . . step on it, faster.'

The man on my right seems about to faint. 'Just look how sick I am . . .' is what he is trying to say. He wants to get back on the trolley.

Once back where we started he says to me, 'I take my hat off to you, Monsieur M. I have never in my life seen in this car anyone who dared egg on Loco Larrea. Were you in the war?'

'No,' I answer with a straight face, 'only in prison.' Still I'm embarrassed. Yet I have lived my life spontaneously, with always new risks. No matter, I shall always be thought a coward.

*

Nightfall found us at Machachi. The car had no lights, not even a headlight. The beam of a dying flashlight shone on the hood (which was red). We had left the escape hatch open. Only now it was he who was urging us on, and cheering. He kept assuring us that we would make it. The speedometer registered 45 m.p.h. Outside I could see nothing but dark. Sometimes, for a second or so, a fleck of moonlight would appear, to be swallowed instantly by a great larvalike cloud. The *loco* knew the road inside out. All of a sudden he would swerve right or left. What is more he was half drunk. Which will it be, I kept thinking, tree or ditch? I made myself as small as I could. No, the road was curving with us. Worse were the bridges which you were only aware of once on them. Whereupon the *loco* would alter his direction. Here the bridges are all narrow. Soon, even though I could not see the road, I felt completely relaxed. Somehow it was like being in a field.

76

On the north road. Quito. Cayumbe. Ontavalo. Ibarra.
The time of the great Indian feast of San Juan at
Ontavalo, which goes on for fifteen days of solid drinking.

July 5.   On the highway, 1 P.M.

Ecuador is immense. But she should show it.
The surroundings of Quito have an *I'd like to but I*
   can't of small copses and shrubs which just gets
                                    in your way.
But the North itself :
'I am naked, yes,

Black and empty, yes,
No trees, no,
No eucalyptus, no,
A few flat aloes is about it
And some huge bits of protuberant earth
And the man who doesn't like it can go elsewhere.
                              O.K. !'

THE LAKE OF SAN PABLO

4 o'clock in the afternoon

Your water ought to be clear.
Whereas you are just very dark.
Most places lakes are joy
Carry rowboats and laughter, dot themselves with cot-
                                    tages.
Whereas you are just dark, dark.
You'd think that at an altitude of 3,900 feet
Any successful lake would come out some form of pink.
You, however, are dark, and, to top that, shallow.
Mount Imbabura has crushed you under her.
She dominates you, and makes you servile.

77

From your shorefront shoots straight for the top, for
                            what's so very much higher
Because she's a large mountain
(Not to mention that she's a large volcano).
She shouts down at you, 'Well!' she shouts, 'Toe!'
Taking on herself at the summit color
To leave you with nothing but the dregs of her shadow.
Oh wretched, oh dark!
Oh! eel-colored lake!

July 7, Ontavalo, and San Pedro

The Indians here, like those elsewhere, for all their dancing, and carousing, and bright-colored dress, do not show in face or gesture any joy whatever. It took a man like the Marquis de Wavrin (who knows America) to tell me: the only ones who laugh are those who do not yet know the white man's oppression.

Saturday, on the way back

Ecuador is one country with some earth to show for itself.

There are not many you can say that for.

No. All over Europe there is that blood-colored laugh of brick houses, roofs and tiles.

And it is covered by that vast oil, its fresh, intense, joyful layer of vegetable green.

Ecuador's earth is brown, black, or lead-colored. That's the tonality of its landscape—and no deviations allowed!

The houses most obviously bear this out, being made of earth and topped with roofs of brown thatch.

Then corn. Corn is not like wheat or sugar cane, no, it is brown.*

You find yourself from a distance saying, 'This is a bare

---

* More precisely it is brown here two-thirds of the year.

mountain.' It is not. It is covered very compactly with corn. Still it has that fire-razed look—the sort of thing that easily passes for so much burnt stubble.

There remains the agave. Out of the ground come a few large leaves in the veiny, livid shape of something about to bloom. Maybe the size of a dog. That's what it is like. And neither the Indian's bread-crust coloring nor the leprous eucalyptus is going to send chuckles through you. There is, however, the poncho. The poncho is the Indian's overcoat. It is something more or less square with a hole in it for the head. What falls down the sides covers the body. This covering is orange, deep red, blue, or violet, striking yet somber colors. It is a calm but definite triumph, one without any bragging or foolery.

But then what are a few triumphs of a square yard in a horizon reckoned only in leagues? Like the industry of some ants in an orchard. No matter how hard they work or what they carry or how intelligent they are, still it is the orchard that you mainly see (unless your specialty is ants).

The Andes! The Andes! They are something to dream about. But they just do not withstand. Not a rock. If something happened, would any one of them hold up? It is only the look that is massive, which is that of a bit of tamed earth, a reserve against the day of its sudden need. An elbow on the table here, a bit of indentation or bomb-spattering or caress or undulation there. The trouble is that each undulation carries a good twenty miles, and any one landscape has at least nine or ten.

In this landscape they are not all there is. In this landscape man is zero. They are ten. The cloud a thousand.

The Ecuadorian cloud—that beauty—does not have an equal anywhere. It does not give ground to any other form, almost completely engulfing the horizon. As for its color, no matter how small it may be (and sometimes you see in a bowl of sky one that is smaller than an eraser, hanging there, shimmering and chameleon in its infinity, and as if at anchor there, oblivious to the wind which has whipped and driven away all the others); as for its color, it comes in every imaginable tint and shade, and defies not only you to match it but every other cloud on this hemisphere, and that includes even the most exceptional of sea clouds.

All of a sudden, how you will never know, around six in the evening it stops. And you do not see another. After that it is a sky of stars. Very pure and dense, almost prickling with stars, and so much more immense than this earth . . .

The star does not light up very much. But to each eye turned its way it sends out its white ray.

DEATH OF A HORSE

Hacienda Guadalupe near Pelileo,
Ambato, 6 A.M., *July 11*

We had just got underway
Suddenly he is dead
He wanted to make a jump
And he is dead
I was up front
And couldn't see anything.
Then Gustave caught up with me.
'And your horse?' I asked astonished
'Well,' he explains, 'He wanted to make a jump
And suddenly he died
I had just enough time to scramble off.'
'Ah! . . .'
Still we're in a hurry; they're awaiting us at the stop
We have to gallop, we get there, and there's the truck
And immediately we have to start off again.
Gustave is embarrassed. He's not to blame.
First the horse had a tremor. Almost instantly he
collapsed.
The two of us slumped in the back, our legs dangling
out.
The trail is starting to climb steeply.
'See that spot, that's he
Down there : he died there where those two trails cross.'
The trail is getting steep.
Meanwhile a huge cloud settles, over the valley,

Keeps settling, is already below us,
Immediately goes to work, with taste,
But in the grand manner,
Shrouding the horse
Under acres of whiteness, as high as it's wide,
And with it every still living horse,
Every colt, steer, various breeds of sheep,
And the hacienda including its pools and brandy re-
serve
We have crossed over a pass
And keep getting farther and farther away
It's on the other side, over there, that the horse died.
Gustave isn't certain whether he died eyes open or
closed
Half-open, he thinks.
Third halt, and still in a hurry, the train is leaving.
Then Gustave says, '*Un gran caballito*,' and that's that
(Which means both a thoroughbred and a damned
good little horse, and what he felt for him)
That's it really, each person thinks, and more besides,
but how do you express yourself fittingly over a
horse?
Horse the color of wheat, whose plumes are the milk
and the wind,
Always restless horse, your head tossing in an ever-
lasting denial
Of protestations, refusals to obey, repeated-in-spite-of-
everything
Of intentions of imminent and undissembled violence—
we-shall-see-now
Actively alert to the aerial mystery
Your head swimming in what's too light to support it
Constantly betrayed by it, constantly swimming
With a display of courage so touching because so futile.
You whom even other horses
Approached only in a certain way
A *gran caballito*, in a word, and he is dead.

WHERE THE JUNGLE BEGINS WHICH GOES ALL THE WAY TO THE SHORES OF THE PACIFIC

Sunday, August 5
On the way out of Saloya

The tree, here, doesn't give a damn for the earth
What counts is to get out and get out fast
Grow tall enough before it suffocates
So off it goes.
No branches, no flowers, no shoots, just a vertical
                trunk
And if a branch comes, it sticks onto the trunk
So as to form an arrow.
Which is
How the *Puma maki* grows,
How the *Arrayan* grows, how the *Cascarilla* with its
                quinine grows,
The *Incienso* with its incense, the *Drago de sangre*
                with its blood
And the *Guarumo* which is white all the way to the
                top, all of them go up,
And when they can't do any more
Having reached the utter limits of their species
Where they can at last let themselves go and spread
                themselves forth in leaves
They're all more or less the same height
And the jungle looks whole.

What it's like is a hundred-yard dash. All of a sudden the runners
are up, sprinting with the one thought of finishing before the
others. And here is the finish line, the one everyone is cheering,
the world record holder, and he ran quite some race. And yet
you look about you flabbergasted, unable to believe your eyes.

Hmmm? How come? Because the whole lot of them have finished within a quarter second of one another.*

> *Friday the 10th, Ecuador's national holiday.*
> *The next day the author, in spite of his known heart trouble, is to undertake the ascent of Mount Atacatzho, 14,742 feet. He does not eat any more, he feels sick, and yet that is what he wanted.*

3 P.M.

I proposed it and they all agreed; it's too late now,
                                    heart, to speak up.
It won't last long, you won't get very tired, I'll be on a
                                    horse;
And it's tomorrow. Today is nothing to worry about.
So why must you from this moment set out to reduce
                                    me, to make me blanch?
To be a fairy, and both dishearten yourself and weaken
                                    me a good deal.
I am playing neither with you nor myself, I know you
                                    both.
But I have made up my mind to know the crater of
                                    Mount Atacatzho.

IN THE CRATER OF MOUNT ATACATZHO 14,742 FEET

Saturday, August 11

Ah! Ah!
Crater?   ah!

---

* Even the fern here realizes that it has to change its ways, its predilection for pavanes and bandage material; it squeezes itself in and stands straight.

We were expecting something more serious . . .
Ah! . . .

It would be nice to come upon something a bit more
                                        serious . . .
Crater?   Indeed? Ah!
We're used to insisting upon something a bit serious.
But what is this laughing valley?
What is this laughing doing here?
These dwarf plant Japanese gardens,
This bit of shaved lawn (because of the awfulness of
                    the climate, of course, but so what?)
This imitation of a flowerbed border? this moss?
And this indoor mildness, this refuge
This picnic site, this springtime
We didn't come here looking for spring
We came to look for a volcano.

Outside, meanwhile, there's a hell of a cold wind blowing—
which shows how high up we are. It angrily erupts down out of
the one existing window in the circular crest, along with all the
chunks of cloud that it has come upon *en route*, and which it
sweeps off whole into the volcano.

Sunday, August 12

Most strange, my heart. I had no ill effects from my mountain climb, and yet some ten doctors have found that I have
heart trouble. Must bring that up in Europe upon my return.

The day after tomorrow ascent of the Corazón, 15,620 feet,
878 feet higher. We shall see what that gives, and perhaps afterward go on to Mount Cotopaxi (19,370 feet).

84

AT PUEMBO

Today in Quito it is being determined whether I am or am not to return to Europe by way of the Amazon.

The descent of the Napo will be by pirogue up to Iquitos, Peru's port on the Amazon. From there on across Brazil by steamer to the Atlantic port of Para.

If yes I shall have to leave in three weeks, because the trip is both long and in its upper reaches not very safe. If it does take place this note is rather beside the point (and actually it is not any too spontaneous). But if it does not I shall at least have this.

*

I shall soon have to leave.

7 P.M., *riding back*

Ecuador, Ecuador, I have not thought that well of you.

Still when about to leave . . . and riding back to the hacienda in a clear moonlight as I am tonight (the nights here are always clear, not too hot, and good for traveling) with Mount Cotopaxi over my shoulder, at 6 : 30 bright pink and now, at this moment, just a dark mass. But for months now I have not looked at it.

Ecuador, all in all you are one hell of a country—but what's going to happen to me?

I'm going back to Paris, and when you return to Paris without a cent a lot of good it will be to have gone back by way of Brazil and the Amazon jungle. Already you feel the cramps of your poverty, and you fidget in spite of yourself over this bug-ridden room which will be a problem finding in this huge Paris which you know, oh, yes, do you ever. For once this is the real truth.

You would think that one or two things about this trip could be ascertained. You would think that yes and no are short words not that hard to pronounce. You would think that a trip requiring four days of hiking, six on horseback, and thirty in a canoe, among still savage tribes and malaria and snakes, and then the crossing of Brazil and the Atlantic, you would think that one might be able to set down a few, very small facts (although I'll admit that you can do quite a number of things in twenty-four hours) . . .

You would think, think, think . . .

One of these days I am going to do the Ecuadorian's portrait.

Wednesday noon, September 12

At 4 P.M. the head bearer is to be paid.

7 P.M.

They are within five hours of Quito? Some news. Gustave, for whom we have to wait so we can do the first four days with him, well, we cannot expect him now before the twenty-fifth. Still, if the head bearer had been paid that would be one thing done, but no. He didn't turn up until afterward, finding me with my head in my hands.

Thursday morning

Now my mind is made up. This whole journey is a trap. Traveling does not broaden you so much as make you sophisticated, 'up-to-date,' taken in by the superficial with that really stupid look of a fellow serving on a beauty prize jury.

The look of a go-getter also. Worth no more. You can just as easily find your truth staring for forty-eight hours at some old tapestry.

REMEMBRANCES

At that time I kept dropping out of sight in that horizon which my two arms contained.

*(The eve of his departure the traveler looks back.
It is as if he were running out of courage.)*

Comparable to nature, comparable to nature, com-
                                        parable to nature,
To nature, to nature, to nature,
Comparable to a feather comforter,
Comparable to thought,
And also in a certain way comparable to the Globe of
                                        the earth,
Comparable to error, to sweetness, and to cruelty
To what is not true, does not stop, to the head of a
                                        driven nail,
To sleep that overtakes you the more surely that you
                                        have been busy elsewhere,
To a song in a foreign tongue,
To a tooth that hurts and remains vigilant,
To the Araucaria that spreads its branches into a patio,
And forms its harmony without sending you a bill, or
                                        giving you an art review,
To the dust there is in summer, to an invalid who
                                        shakes
To the eye losing a tear and so cleansing itself,
To clouds superimposed, foreshortening the horizon
                                        but making you think of the sky.
To the glow of a station at night, when you arrive not
                                        knowing if there are any more trains.
To the word Hindu, for someone who never went
                                        where you find them in every street,
To what is related about death,
To a sail in the Pacific,

To a hen underneath a banana leaf, one rainy after-
noon,
To the caress of a great weariness, to a long-dated
promise,
To the bustle of a nest of ants,
To the wing of a condor when the other wing is already
at the opposite slope of the mountain,
To certain combinations,
To the marrow bone at the same time as to a lie,
To a young bamboo at the same time as to the tiger
who squashes the young bamboo.
Comparable to me finally,
And even more to what is not me.
By, you who were my *By* . . .

Thursday

Our departure postponed to the 25th.

Noon Thursday

Postponed to the 28th.

The big struggle is with their family doctor. Like a deaf man
he keeps shouting that he won't be held responsible for my
death. My rotten health, he says, my liver, my heart trouble.

This, naturally, does not do much to put people at ease.

To top it off my sinus condition is coming back. The left part
of my nose is so stopped up that you would think herring fillets
had been somehow slipped up it. I stubbornly insist that it's
nothing, only to show up this morning with my eye half closed as
a result of the inflammation.

With all this we are given the *names* of the last White people
drowned in the Napo, along with those of the district's man-
eating (?) tribes.

O.K., but a lot of good *that* does once you are there. Here they have all gone berserk over this trip.

We are leaving tomorrow afternoon. I had the tooth broken which was giving me the sinus. Half of it has remained in my jaw, and since we have no dog *it* will keep watch at night, and during the day it will help keep me curbed in. Participation in nature, flowing admiration—let's not count on all this. It will not let anything by but the very best, what is solid. With the same of course true for all one's worries and harms.

Still I shall have to keep it under control.

It has got a pocket of pus on its side.

O.K., but I have a lancet and I am taking it with me.

Thursday

Tomorrow departure of our Yumbos with our main baggage (Yumbos: Indians from the East).

Friday, 11 A.M.

They are to leave on the train from Ambato at 12 : 30.

Friday, noon

Their departure put off until Saturday.

Our own departure has been likewise put off until 8 A.M., Monday, by car.

It may well be that my life up to now may have been somewhat deficient on the courage side.

Deficient, and perhaps courage was what conditioned my life,
what gave it that feeling I have always had of being unem-
ployed and hence available.

Deficient mainly in the sense of adequate occasions.

Deficient in its understanding of courage, and its respect for
this element.

Saturday, September 23, noon

The departure of our Yumbos has been put off until noon,
Monday, October 1.

Saturday, 1 P.M.

The Yumbos will leave Monday morning in a truck with our
baggage.

Many Frenchmen once they have made a promise before
witnesses feel obligated by their word.

Well, not the Ecuadorian. He has said tomorrow, very well it
will be the day after that. And when you await him two days
later, oh no, it is over with, or rather something else, or nothing
at all. *He has changed his mind.*

When it comes to matters of form he does not put his word to
one side.

No, he changes his mind, his word, it is all the same.

This is the cause for our numerous postponements, and for my
months of unease.

Departure.
Arrived at Guadalupe.

The luggage has not arrived.
They missed the only train of the week.

Arrival of the luggage by mule.

Look for bearers.
No bearers.

Found a few mules for as far as Méra.

Departure for Méra.
There will be four of us and a guide as far as Méra.
There will be three of us as far as Napo.
And two beyond there—me and A. de Monlezun. Gustave is leaving us when we reach the Napo River.

Trail with nothing but sheer precipice on its right and so narrow that you are constantly taking your foot out of the stirrup and lifting up your leg so it will not be crushed against some tree or rock : for the horse seeing the precipice to the right tries to keep as close as he can to the mountain. We fear for the mules. They are carrying a double load, which snags easily . . .

Among the local birds at this time was a bottle popper. His song is not very lengthy. A note, first, of preparation, then *bzzap* . . . at which point the cork flies out of your bottle and the liquor gushes out foaming. What was most brilliantly mimicked was the tearing off of the cork : you sensed both the ensuing void and the air as it rushed back down the neck. I tried to keep my mind off it. Hopeless.

This jungle with its champagne popping all about us was stupendous.

Méra

Noon arrival.
No bearers.
We are leaving tomorrow for Satzayacu (four days of hiking with no trail), from where we'll send out for bearers.

Next day

Departure.
Alfred Mortensen kept telling us, 'Hah ! hah ! hah ! You'll see,

you won't manage a single day, you'll have to backtrack. It isn't for you, this, mud up to your stomach.'

He was riding a bit behind. He wanted to come with us to where we made our first fording. But he went down in the mud. We just kept going. That's the last we have heard of him.

*

A Dutchman, a settler at Napo, is ahead of us with piles of luggage. He had one of his trunks crushed and smashed open by a falling tree. We could see that he was taking his dinner jacket with him. If it blows any harder we are going to have to stop. Our Yumbos say it is too dangerous, too many dead trees.

What we really need is a drink. But the liquor chest is behind at Méra, along with the rest of our luggage.

*

During most of these four days both A. and I kept covertly watching one another. Is he going to hold out? each of us was thinking.

To hold out, I could see him walking with this one thought. An inner concentration was in each one of his steps. It gave him the startling look of a prophet. After those four days I never once saw that expression on him. In all his life he may never have it again.

Reached Satzayacu.

MÉRA-SATZAYACU (NAPO)

October 16

This hike takes place in the desert.
This desert is a forest.
Four days of roots and slime.
No birds, no serpents, no mosquitoes.

93

The ground is cold and everywhere swamp.
All the same it's the tropical forest.
Enough just to see its ostentation, that look of a dressed-
up whore.
But what this most resembles is a sewer.

There is no path and you go on foot.
Stumble foot! stumble! blister!
The wet soil doesn't give a damn, says neither yes nor
no,
Gargles fatly,
And receives you up to your waist.
Stumble! Stumble! Made ridiculous!
The root stumps tear into you,
Smash and break your toe,
Sticking, make you slip, jounce you,
Knock you down, eliminate you,
And lose you in one of those never-ending slimy holes
That form the jungle floor.
Worse still I'm sensitive to the cold.
At night I shivered horribly.
I thought I had malaria.

Satzayacu. Chaves' cabin

G., A., and I were assigned a single apartment.

Chaves is popular with the Indians. All those passing by climb
up to his cabin and come to shake hands with him—bringing
their wives.

When you hire Indians as rowers, first they give you their
hands, then you haggle.

The young Indian girl who keeps house for Chaves goes to the
brook often to fetch water.

On her way back she realizes I am there, eyeing her. She turns
her head my way, spits briskly, and smiles. There is a wonderful
sort of health and joy in that gesture. It is also, in its way, a

greeting. Which makes me want to spit in reply. Only . . . I spit so badly.

One day she came near. I asked her to paint her skin. And she was quite ready to. She kept giggling, all the while looking as though she were soothing a child.

Then quite suddenly she left. Indian men are extremely jealous.

First trip by pirogue

To get to Napo we borrowed the men and pirogue of the Salvador ranch. The *bogas* (rowers) were nice-looking men but lousy *bogas*. They could never make up their mind which arm of the stream to take.

At one bend the *popero* (the bowman) fell overboard. It was not noticed until much later, when someone asked him, 'Right or left?' His head was four hundred yards back, and the only thing above water.

The stream was shallow. Occasionally we would find ourselves stopped short, as if seized by a hand.

Shooting the rapids—and on the Satzayacu these come every three hundred yards—the canoe hurtled along the bottom like a man on his back falling down a staircase. We were completely drenched by lots of tiny furious waves splashing against the sides.

The Chuntunyacu rushing into the Satzayacu forms the Napo. It rushes in like a lunatic, and its current sweeps across from one end to the other. And there the two streams slug it out. The entire surface is chopped into waves, and you think you have reached the ocean. Once formed, the Napo falls.

Entering the current was like a ripping of gears. The shock of it knocked me on my back as I was about to hand G. his camera. Lying there at the bottom of the pirogue I would have sworn it was undulating.

Once we had got through the junction we had to bail quickly, for the water was right up to our bow.

The town of Napo is a quarter of an hour farther on.

That afternoon we arrived in Napo Port for the first time. We counted seven cabins. There were a few more pirogues. Say a dozen. The most sizable building had on it a large inscription : *Jefatura política.*

The prefect greeted us. After acknowledging the letter from the minister which we brought with us, he had some sacks full of God knows what cleared out of the room where we were to sleep. We remained with him in another, which was completely open. There was a vampire bat flying back and forth between us and the roof. And there was a Victrola. They kept winding it up and reloading it for us even during the meal. I really wondered what I was doing there. The air kept getting thicker. What the Victrola was doing was obvious : supplying the two Dutch settlers and the prefect with white women. You could feel it invoking them. But why, if they liked women that much, didn't they go back to the capital?

Soon we excused ourselves. The Victrola stopped, and the first thing we knew the brush had sprung up all around us. Down below the river was making its own noise. Tomorrow, flood.

We went into the room that had been prepared for us. Automatically before undressing, you take out your flashlights and shine them on the walls. This done I lit myself a cigarette. 'Boy, what a mess!' A. exclaimed, and G. must have laughed. He has the sort of young laugh that goes well anywhere.

We then faced the situation before us. There were something like two or three hundred hairy spiders, each about the size of a wad of tobacco, perched there, each on his own hole of shadow. This texture hardly shifted at all.

A. kept insisting that we keep the candles lit all night (A. is a daredevil, but the one thing he does not care for is little crawling beasts).

G. and I got out our machetes and started to flail away at the lot. Thick gooky pieces came down all over, heads, two or three legs here, four or five there. A number of bleeding abdomens managed somehow to retire behind bits of bamboo. To get at the spiders on the ceiling you had to hold on to the machete with both hands (because the machete, though no longer than a saber, is both wider and thicker and for that reason weighs more). One of you holds the flashlight, the other hits—and hits hard (you have to, because the bamboo recedes and retreats along with the spider). Blows to take the fuzz off a monkey's head, and every spider quakes. But retreat, no, never. Only those wounded leave.

We had to make sure that on the first whack they did not drop onto our sleeves. As for the beds A., kept a watch over them. After a good two hours most of the spiders were back outside, some dying, others . . . A. was worried about these others. But G. and I felt full of energy.

*

Napo-Téna, on horseback

The prefect tells us that the only time there are steamships at Rocafuerte is during the rice harvest. He has no idea if the harvest is going on right now.

They had an Italian bishop there—a good businessman.

We have a somewhat errant father, he says, it is quite possible you will run into him in the course of your trip. The tone in which he speaks about him shows his discomfort. Obviously he does not absolve him.

But I know this missionary. The sort who, no matter what the weather, will travel ten days to be by an Indian's sickbed. So like a damn idiot I tell the bishop, 'Monsignor, Jesus has forgiven so many of them. Those he could bear were walking tombs.'

A chill fell. The bishop is hard of hearing, so I had spoken loudly. Yet the only reply was his parrot's raucously insistent, '*Que? que? que dice?*' (what, what, what's that you're saying?).

Without G's coming in to take a picture with his *Pathé baby* I don't know how it would have ended.

*

97

Brazilian missionaries are not exactly the best sort. One whose relations with women were notorious was told, 'But really, Father, you're not being very ecclesiastic.'

'Oh,' he replied, with a beautiful smile, 'what we need are baptisms . . .'

On the other hand, it is difficult to convert Indians completely to Christianity. Christ for them is not someone to look up to, he is all right, but he does not satisfy them. They didn't seem to value kindness very highly. At any rate they are far removed from the Jew.

Back at Satzayacu

High flood. We have difficulty heading against the current. Twelve hours to make twenty-five miles.

There we look for bearers to go fetch the baggage left behind. We need fourteen.

Seven show up.

There are five others on the other side of the stream.

Two then are missing.

Which of the crates should we sacrifice?

Today, the Indians' scheduled departure.

At eight A.M. they are still around. It is raining. If at six that morning it has rained, the Indian will not leave, it brings bad luck. However, it rains here approximately eighteen hours a day.

Next day: Sunday

Sunday is a bad day. White Man's day. Brings bad luck. Do not leave.

Monday, finally, they depart.

Eight days later, return of only three bearers; an hour later, four more. They say the others will not be here before tomorrow.

Next day, three more bearers. Two missing. These arrive in the evening.

*

Our rowers for the Napo arrive. Six rings apiece and two for their wives; this plus the yard or two of cloth that each needs to wrap around his middle, and twenty 1-sucre notes ($20.00). The Indian only recognizes the 1-sucre note. If you give him a 100-sucre note, he will perforce take it for 2 sucres. It is the amount of paper that counts. Also you need bags to put his money in.

The monetary unit: the strip of cloth and the 1-sucre note.

They only speak Quechua. I know a few words, not that much.

Tomorrow departure.

First day in the pirogue.
Satzayacu, October 22
Napo. Vargas Torres

Too small and mobile a pirogue. Several times just missed tipping over.

The prefect at Napo has us take another one, much longer, which has just come in from Rocafuerte.

My travel mate, A., not wishing to lose time, says that it is not worth the trouble. The prefect, however, insists, insists with a kind of maniacal fear.

O.K., we accept. You see he is relieved. I just kept cold-bloodedly looking at him. In his eyes' fear there was mainly the minister. The minister was there, he was raising his finger and saying, 'Prefect of Napo, fired!'

Latas

The rapids reputed the most dangerous. Worse still we keep having to get out and haul the pirogue.

Up to now we have had to pray for 'no flood.' Now the river gets deep and much slower, and we have to pray for floods.

The administrator, a real invalid. His movements are quick but tremulous. You gather that he has to keep a grip on himself so as not to go mad. We offer him whisky. Afterward we have dinner. And there he is talking always faster and faster. The words sail out of him. A. says to me, 'He's going to beat his own record, wait and see.' The words pop out, one after another. For some time I have not understood a thing. When he laughs the bursts of laughter come so fast that you wonder whether you are not watching a circus number.

Before we go we leave with him two tubes of quinine.

He tells us that at Rocafuerte we will find everything we need. He himself has never been there.

Next day

This stretch is a long one, the Indians were to come for us at five this morning. However it is raining.

Departure at 8 A.M.

I pass away what time I have near the stable. There are some very pretty birds there. Quite long-legged, like flamingos, and pink, with wings of a soft gray. In all about the size of a pigeon. I really wanted one, but once you take them captive they die.

—Cross over and get us some banana leaves, there are lots of them there on the right bank.

For two hours now we have had a torrential downpour.

But no, they don't want to. The right bank is the bank of the *infieles* (heathen), which is what they call the Jivaros. The Jivaros go about naked and with their spears attack anything non-Jivaro and kill it, women aside. A woman can come in handy.

Occasionally they come over to the left bank. What they do then, since they do not own pirogues, is swim across gripping their spears. They live in the territory extending between the Napo (i.e., the right bank) and the Pastaza.

O.K., but we are soaking wet, those are nice leaves over there that will make us a perfectly decent shelter. Will you fetch us some!

We get angry, but even so nothing happens.

We give them some spirits to drink, and things get a little better. But we still have to be there while they are picking, our rifle and two revolvers trained on the great jungle canopy.

But I say to A., if these Jivaros come along, what are we to do?

For me, he answers, that would be simple. Five bullets for them and the sixth for me (and he is a man of his word). I have no wish to become one of those people's funny experiences. I couldn't take it.

And I . . . well, that word 'experience' has me thinking. For me, too, it would be one to live with these savages, and not necessarily the one he has in mind. I am convinced I would try living with them.

Reached Arménia

The hacienda of Don Nicolas Torres. The district king. Only he is feeling depressed. His son has just died of the fever.

After the meal someone signals me to go into the next apartment. An old man is there in his death throes. An Italian singer. And beside himself to be talking French. Only he more rasps than he speaks. Every other second you have to relight his cigarette, which gives off an odor of the church. We brought him valerian and a bottle of ether. He took it and peered at it quite closely.

We have been informed that the motor barge will be in Rocafuerte in about twenty-five days.

Third day by pirogue

We started rowing at 4 A.M., pushing ourselves to reach Ribadeneira's cabin, the only one on the route.

By the time we docked it had been dark for two hours. The way to the dwelling place lay through a swamp.

We ask for a place to stay.

But R. himself seemed fidgety.

Our Indian began cooking up a mess of turtle eggs. Yet it was not till they were on our plates, along with some fried bananas, that Ribadeneira made up his mind to speak out.

To have gone back on board would have made more sense. They had something like *vomito-negro* raging here. It killed you in three hours. He had spent the day digging graves for his Indians—fourteen of them.

'Si Señor,' the survivors called, four or five white heads poking out of a kind of hayloft.

'So they couldn't wait for us to have finished eating!' A. said.

Horribly true. Eating is not that natural. One must first be in a somewhat hopeful state of mind.

I went right to bed. What I need most now is to get my head clear and meditate.

*

Ribadeneira says there is a sloop leaving Rocafuerte for Iquitos eight days from now. We ordered rice bags from him for that date.

Tomorrow morning, departure.

Fourth day in the pirogue

DEATH OF A MONKEY

He was watching us. I shouldered. 'In the head!' the Indian shouted. But his look threw me off. I fired the bullet into his chest. There was a piercing, sad, almost womanlike cry. He was not really that big. Then he fell onto a lower branch. For one moment he seemed to be dancing. But he was dead. We had to go unclench his grip. Then our Indian carried him in his arms to the pirogue. The pair of us looked like thieves.

We started off again, after laying him down under some banana leaves. From time to time I would take them off. All the while he kept up his look of alert good company.

When we tied up he was still warm. There had been a strong sun all day.*

Fifth day in the pirogue

Reached the Victoria ranch.

If you climb to the roof you can see Rocafuerte and across the way the Peruvian garrison town of Pantoja.

*

The farmer says there is no sloop now at Rocafuerte, and should one come it can be heard from here. He invites us to stay. It is the one place in the district, he says, with no malaria.

Next day

Just before leaving I find a little girl of twelve to thirteen, dressed in pink and quite serious looking, watching me as I fold my bedding and hand it to the Indian.

'I didn't see you, little girl, yesterday. Where were you?'

'In the house.'

'But why weren't you around, you pretty little thing?'

With that she came up and held out her palm.

---

* On a day that I can't place in my memory we had to leave behind the pirogue and our Indian boatmen, who were not able to go on any farther. The waters had swollen. The way back against the current was going to take them a long time, about a month.

We had now before us a much longer stretch than anticipated. After sorting out the advice given us, and a good deal of hesitation, we ended up taking passage in the pirogue of a Portuguese businessman known as *the Jew*, a man of doubtful reputation who was openly treated with scorn. The pirogue was big enough, but slow, not very maneuverable, and overloaded.

Once started it is obvious that we can't trust him. Our relations get bad. We have the feeling that he would stick us there, if presented with the chance. [Footnote added to 1968 edition]

'Oooh!'

White palm—malaria—she must have had an attack yesterday. That's why she was so serious and, moreover, so pale.

'You've never had malaria?' she asks.

'No,' I reply, tenderly, 'but it will come sure enough.'

They were calling for me.

'I'll be soon going to Iquitos,' she adds.

The current out of Victoria is rough, and got us off right
away.

*

Five years ago this rancher was quarantined in a leper's camp.
He managed to escape. One day wandering about the edge of
his property he encounters an Indian of his who is in perfect
health. The point is, they were both lepers and had been
quarantined together.

'A snake stung me,' the Indian explains. 'After a high fever I
quickly got well.'

So they go off looking for snakes of this kind.

All very well. But the snake doesn't want to bite. He needed a
few kicks in the head.

AT ROCAFUERTE ON THE AGUARICO BORDER
BETWEEN PERU AND ECUADOR

Having had our fill of quinine, heat, the rocking of the
pirogue, the Amazon jungle with its dense, never-ending foliage,
the huge stretch of water both in back and ahead of us—ahead
malaria mostly, and it is nothing, just yellow fever—and there is
nothing to do but keep going ahead into it for the next thirteen
days, hollow-headed, your heart like a piece of glue, and your
lungs and stomach flat.

What a mess!

The author having done some 316 miles in a canoe had the
notion of finding at Rocafuerte a motor launch, only it will not

leave for another month, and so he will continue on down the Napo to where it joins the Amazon, covering some 875 miles in a canoe, stuck under a *pamakari* which is a roof deck made out of cambered leaves reaching all the way down to the water line, coffin heated at 98 degrees with nothing there but rice sacks which you bump against, you cannot read or do anything, you are lying there completely prone, and a filthy Brazilian Jew has undertaken to get us to our destination. It will be great! To top it off both the author's feet and his left leg are beginning to show ugly signs of gangrene. His dosage of *café ispirine* is already at six tablets a day, he feels terrible and has a hard time walking. It is a local ailment, the better care he takes, the more it spreads. It comes from the *issang*. It looks a lot like leprosy.

Saturday, November 3, in the pirogue
suffering and probably with a temperature

Give me greatness,
Give me greatness,
Give me slowness,
Give me slowness,
Give me everything,
And give me yourself,
And give again—
Even then it won't be enough.

Despair is sweet—
Sweet to the point of vomit.
And I'm really scared.
When I'm chilled to the very marrow
Yes, I'm scared, scared
I'm no more, I hardly exist.

Please friend—
I'm hanging onto your memory,
Onto your height.

I'm hanging but falling,
I let go.
So I wasn't as much myself as I had been told.
I'm living upside down.
One more day? Two?
And Iquitos is still twelve days off.

*

Forced yesterday by a sudden nightfall to tie up at a *playa* (a sandy island out in mid-river). There we were in full storm, in the most incredible downpour, with a rapidly rising tide that kept battering against the *playa* (bits of it kept crumbling all around and splattering us), and which threatened to deluge it entirely; without light, almost without arms; in mortal peril, moreover, of *la boa**—the boa rises up out of the water and makes its way down into the tunnel of the *pamakari* (where we are trying to sleep on tightly packed rice sacks hard as stones), the boa enters, takes what is edible, rolls it up, and with it re-enters the water; also in peril of suddenly being set loose and knocked against one of the Napo's numerous dead trees—huge things brandishing a mass of slippery branches as they crash about in mid-current; in peril of being tossed into the jungle swarming as it is with jaguars and *tigrillos*, with serpents including the *vibora chuchupi*, the most frightening of the lot since it only comes out at night and is no bigger than your arm and cackles like a hen; during the day it stays in a hole it has made; but if it has been too busy to make itself a hole before the night's end it spends the next day wherever it is, its coils piled one over the other, and sleeping; in peril of a greater poisoner still,† the *chuchora machacu*, one of those bugs called gold-

---

* The Spaniard says *la* boa, the Frenchman *le* boa. It doesn't take long to figure out which is right.

In the Aguarico everyone verified the story of the tribesman who had been borne away by boas, but the cases are rare.

† According to various reports that only later we knew to be quite false; the insect is scary-looking but harmless. [Footnote added to 1968 edition]

beaters that has the shape—it's weird—of a hippopotamus' head (the same insignificant tiny black eyes set far back on its head), half blind, and which flies about with its stinger in front inserting it deeply wherever there is resistance, and while impaled emitting a fatal liquid.

In the midst of the piercing police sirens of the parakeets (*loras* and *guacamayos*), squawk-squawk! Loud, everywhere, and long-winded—with that inhuman sound of struck bronze—among them *cotos* (big dark monkeys), and it's with his howls that the *macho* pelts the *hembra*, our Indian explains.

Good Lord, something at last! It broke up the monotony of a canoe day which is not to be believed. I am talking about an *embalsada* canoe, i.e., one bordered with floats, two enormous logs which help support the cargo, and heavy in proportion. Barely able to maneuver, you let the current take you along, no faster and no slower, wherever it goes, to the right or to the left (and this in a river that is often over two miles wide).

November 2

We will never make it with this pirogue, it fails to make headway. With these balsa logs on its sides it's impossible.

Evening. Reached a Peruvian's hut.

'What a misfortune,' he suddenly said to me, 'that Christopher Columbus was the one to discover America. In his wake there came droves of Spaniards. Germans would have been preferable, *gente trabajadora.**' Out of politeness he adds, 'Or the French.'

He was, however, a pure Castilian.

His definition of the Spaniard: a quarreler, a card sharp, and a thief.

It was not long before he had won all my Peruvian money in a poker game. He also got into a quarrel with the Jew. He was, thus, short of being a Spaniard only by a third, since he stole nothing from us.

* Workers.

107

In spite of the hurricane lights there are vampire bats flying all around us.

I have no idea why I suddenly get up and turn on my flashlight. I go back to bed. A little later I get up once more. It seems to be raining—my sheets are red with blood to the depth of my knees. Drops of blood are falling from the hammock overhead.

The danger with vampire bats is that they will drain you before you feel it—by what anesthetic it is hard to say, all the while beating their wings. Once fed they go away, but you go on bleeding.

The boy's feet are bandaged, after which he is wrapped up tightly in his bed clothes. And forbidden to stir.

Once you have been stung they can pick you out of a throng, and it is you they want.

Cattle who have been left out often wake in the morning anemic and drunk, and wobbly-footed.

*Junction of the Curare River with the
Napo River. 2da. guarnición peruana**

A Palisada.
From far off we could see and hear the huge logs sleeping out in the river. Now a rough current was driving us toward them. Some we avoided. Others we nudged our way past. There were some strung out all the way across this arm of the Napo, and farther on downstream for at least 100 yards. Finally we saw the one that was going to get us. It looked as if it had just at that moment risen from the water. The balsa log that was our left float was thrown in the air. A sack of rice toppled into the river, the demijohn of brandy smashed, and the *tartaruga* (one of those big 200-pound tortoises) which was on its back turned over and bit me on the shoe. The pirogue tipped. We were half underwater (without the two balsa logs floating our right and left the pirogue would have gone to the bottom just from the weight of its cargo) when miraculously the tree trunk as it came down

---

* Second Peruvian fort. [Translator's note]

managed to jam itself between two neighboring logs.

We still tipped badly to our left, the tortoise was kicking furiously and had split open the sacks, out of which rice poured like milk. We were able to make land some five minutes later.

Reached M.'s farm. We meet there a Colombian

C.   You have been with this humbug of a Jew for how many days?

Me.   Twelve days.

C.   You have been making short days, right?

Me.   No, fourteen-hour days, but the pirogue doesn't seem to get anywhere.

C.   At that rate it will take you another four or five days to get to Mazan.

Me.   Our Jew says two days.

C.   That's crazy, four at the least because he has to make detours. It is impossible for him loaded as he is to ride with the current.

Me.   Oh!

C.   Me, if I had my men and the pirogue here I could get you there in a day. And from there it's only a half day to Iquitos.

A. gives me a look. He is covered with boils from head to toe. They came on all at once. He would just as soon be under a doctor's care. Me. 'O.K.'

Me.   Where are your men and the pirogue?

C.   Twelve miles from here, and on the road, what's more, to Mazan.

Me.   Can you possibly get hold of them?

C. to V.   Do you have a pirogue here?

V.   No.

C. to Z.   Do you have a pirogue?

Z.   No, but go see D., he has one.

C.   I have a pirogue.
Me.   Great! Tomorrow, then, at what time?
C.   Three hours from now. The men must leave for work at six
o'clock. We'll have to be at my place beforehand. So be ready
by 2 A.M.
Me.   Good.

The cattle are lowing, and seem to be much closer to the
hacienda. It is a bright night. Before long you see a man
approach, he's just killed a jaguar. His son has stayed below to
clean it. As proof the man brought along the teeth. Shattered, the
jaguar's teeth fell out, and he merely had to pick them up. Here
they are.

Our bags are removed from the Jew's pirogue and placed in
the other. It is cold. The sky is getting more and more overcast.
'Do you think there'll be a storm?'
'Is a storm in the offing?'
It is a question I ask every other moment. Because there is no
pamakari, and thus no shelter. At any event the waves would be
too high for our pirogue, which is a small one. The sky is not
getting any clearer, but then it is not getting any more overcast.
It will do. There are a few stars out. A great murmuring which
is like silence. With regularity the oar dips into the water, and
drinks.
The Napo divides here into three great waterways. They are
all equal, and grand, and for hours at a stretch absolutely
straight. Each is about a half mile wide. You wonder what there

will be at the end : a big screen grating? the Last Judgment?
Arrived at 5 :45 A.M.
Left again at 7 A.M.
Arrived in Mazan at seven that evening.

The merging of the Amazon with the Napo is still a day
farther on. But there is a shortcut through the jungle that allows
you to reach a branch of the Amazon in an hour's walk. After
that it is just one more day back up the river to Iquitos.
Me.   Can you get us four porters for tomorrow? and a pirogue
    to Iquitos?
X.   Yes.

*

André and I make pretty funny travelers. Malaria . . . hell!
We just want to go to sleep. Our mosquito nets are small. They
make you suffocate, and we have never used them. But here
there are decidedly too many mosquitos. Sleepless night.

Next day, 7 A.M.

We.   Are our men ready?
X.   I'll take a look.
We.   Well?
X.   No. Out of the question. There is no pirogue on the other
    side. But my son should be back right away.
We.   Makes no difference. We're leaving. Maybe we'll find a
    canoe on the other side.
X.   No, they're all out, it's Sunday.
We.   That's O.K. We'll wait on the other side.

A. and I have one principle we stick to, which is all we really know about this part of the world : you must, whenever possible, go on to the stop ahead, no matter how silly it looks; don't wait where you are.

Seeing us determined they begin looking upriver for a pirogue, and we head for the other side. Around ten o'clock the pirogue is there.

9 P.M. *Arrived at Iquitos*

It was night when we got into Iquitos. The current was so strong that even with everyone rowing we remained in place. We had to hug the bank very closely.

It was full of wooden footbridges. Certain low ones—intended for little boats—had to be raised so that our *pamakari* could pass under.

From high up in the freighters the lookouts watched suspiciously as we glided by. The moment our baggage was set down on the dock our rowers took off (because any stranger found in Iquitos is grabbed and put to manual labor for fifteen days).

Three weeks from now there will be a Brazilian boat to take us all the way down the Amazon to Para (on the Atlantic).

IQUITOS, PERU, PORT ON THE AMAZON

November 15

What makes the bourgeois is his daily régime. It happens the world over. However one man's régime may utterly undo a man of the other régime, i.e., the stranger, and this no matter how meek and boring and everyday this same régime is for the native.

In the daily régime of this country there is the *issang*. You wade into some wet grass. You are itching in no time. Already there are some twenty at your feet, hardly visible except through a magnifying glass, little red dots but pinker than blood.

You become alarmed, you curse, you get yourself infected, you call for anything—tiger, puma—but what you get is just the régime.

Another régime item : very small mosquitoes. They sting hardly at all, nest in your eyebrows, there only, by the hundreds . . .

You call for a boa but what you get is the daily régime.

One thing more : the water here has a charming tiny fish, about as big as a thread of wool—pretty, transparent, and gelatinous.

You bathe, and it comes up to you, seeking to penetrate you.

After having with much sensitivity probed you to your innermost point (it adores natural orifices), now its one idea is to get out. It backs up a bit; then in spite of itself, two needlelike fins come flaring out. It gets anxious and moves around, and so, open umbrella style and trying to wedge its way out, it manages to rip you into any number of hemorrhages.

Either you succeed in poisoning the fish or you die.

But a more likely end is this one : the moment blood spreads in the water, no matter how small the amount, *caneros* come. They are not much larger than sardines and just as numerous, and differ only in their strength and voracity, being capable of carrying off your finger in a single movement. A 150-pound man or woman will take them, on the average, 10 minutes.

There has never been a corpse recovered from the Amazon.

Nor has there ever been a corpse found in the Amazon.

*

I have seldom heard the Tropics discussed matter-of-factly. It's scarcely possible. You go forward here like police detectives. Simply to sit down you have to take laboratorylike precautions. Whereas in Europe you can give yourself up to the outdoors, and exist with it on equal terms.

As for owning property here . . . What then? The serpent comes and kills you in your own home.

There may well be a whole jungle around me. But because of the immense heat all I hear is my veins singing. Rather monotonous song. But still a song very much my own, and I listen to it all day long.

When the sun sets there is a bit of breeze. But then it is night and you cannot see a thing.

*

I have in me a strong propensity to intoxication. I am a man obsessed, and everything is my meat. Thus, when I read, the first pages hold no interest for me. They are too straightforward. But after a few hours it all gets fluid, and I then find a real pleasure.

The trees here are well lit up and luminous. I do not see them, I only see their glow. My eyes are always wide open like a baby's, and like a baby I only turn them when something shifts in front of me.

I cannot very well explain myself. While it is true that I speak more often about what bothers me, I also have my share of little delights.

*

I am now very sorry I did not kill that Brazilian Jew who was to have taken us to Iquitos. Every chance we had of doing him in would also have forced us to kill the kid who was with him.

There was one storm-filled night on the river when we narrowly missed being swept away. Our hands on the trigger, my companion and I each had the same thought. If the pirogue slips its mooring he gets his brains blown out. On that we could not be more in agreement.

*

The advice you are given before setting out on an exploration has a great deal in common with that given to children.

One man may counsel modesty; others, 'Be ambitious'; another, 'Don't be too ambitious,' or, 'Be frank,' 'Be prudent,'

114

'Courageous,' 'Use your head.' However what the child needs to know is not that *a person* can succeed by being either modest or tolerant or courageous. What counts is whatever is easiest for *him*; it is up to him to decide whether pride or modesty will get him furthest. The same holds for this trip. I was given an endless amount of advice, most of it contradictory. But I now know what will do for me. I'm not going to say it, but I know.

*

Iquitos

In the street a little girl, maybe five or six years old, comes up to you. '*Mama le llama*' ('Mommy want to speak to you'), she takes you sweetly by the hand and leads you to her mother.
And Mama . . . Mama . . . well, it's two sols ($4.00).

*

Departure on the Victoria

We will be in Manaus ten days from now and in Para in sixteen.

Not a tall boat, but as wide as the *Majestic*.

We do not recognize the Amazon; we are tourists now.

The boat stops every twelve hours to take on wood. At the same time it takes on its quota of heat and mosquitos. The young blades of the vicinity come aboard to have their locks cut by the ship's barber, who announces, 'In the latest style of Paris and Rio de Janeiro.'

We also sail at night. There are searchlights. We do not turn them on. They disturb the pilot.

The bottom of the Amazon like the current is constantly shifting. You can sometimes remain aground for three or four weeks. The more you push the deeper in you get.

*

Manaus (38° C. heat). Brazil

All along the right bank of the river for about a mile an enormous, very high wall. Behind and above it—Manaus.

This town of 100,000 is 1,200 miles from everything, and any road you take, at the end of it there is just the jungle.

The local people regard their town as a heap of rubble. Yet indications of wealth are everywhere—a Big City theater as well as some new monuments. In a small neighborhood theater you read, 'Here in 1911 Pavlova danced.' The pound sterling was then small change, but the rubber prices fell and now there are only memories.

*

A long time ago when I was a child I came upon a rod. At a certain level it suddenly swelled into two teats. It was still a rod, but there, on the spot, it had turned feminine.

The women here are slender, very slender. But once at the chest life unclenches and goes wild. Perfect breasts, under the brassière braced and ready. And like the white girls the Negresses come big, their breasts the same.

The French chargé d'affaires explained it as a vice they are prone to while among themselves.

*

There was a formal reception at the church that went on until quite late. The women were in full décolleté, the men in white or black dinner jackets. *Os homens deven*, the preacher shouted ('the men should'), but you could hardly hear him. There were chairs scattered about in small laughing groups. Along the steps of the side altars some girls had sat down, holding onto each other's shoulders. Sometimes the last in a row would slide down a step, followed by a mad burst of never-ending giggling.

Os homens deven, the preacher insisted. We were stuck together, each to the next, while a constant wave swept the mass of bodies. The cause was a stream of youngsters who kept circulating, trying to find someone they could push against and enrage.

From time to time people went up in groups to take refreshment at the bar of the Blessed Virgin. There was also in the square a traveling fair with gambling of all sorts. And the noise of the betting shot into the church like whips.

*

To tell the truth, at Iquitos I was already beginning to have my fill. I'd have liked to go unobserved; to make myself very small and arrive in Paris where I could hide myself in my books.

But soon I would wake up with still all Brazil to be crossed.

Which is one reason why this looks like the twentieth time I've been on this one trip.

And it's becoming one tedious . . .

*

The Amazon isn't like the Napo
The Napo swims slowly toward the Amazon
Slowly.
Home again.
Worn out.
Above it there blows an unquestionable wind.
Oh! the wind!

I'm from a country of wind
In my country even the poorest has his wind
The air is never harvested, it puffs, that's wind,
We always have a lot, and we need it—wind! wind!

The man who has grown up
Who has spent years in the passionate hand of the wind

I'd no idea I was this attached to my country
But this wind . . .
The wind . . .

THE AMAZON WASN'T ABOUT TO LET ITSELF BE SEEN BEFORE THE TWENTIETH CENTURY

Para, December 15.* Mouth of the Amazon

Lots of narrow passages, 1/2 mile to 1 1/4 mile wide, and that's it.†

But where is the Amazon, you ask, and yet you never get to see any more than that.

You have to go up. You need an airplane. So I have not seen the Amazon. And I won't talk about it.

A young woman who was on our boat, coming from Manaus, went into town with us this morning. When she came upon the Grand Park (which is undeniably nicely planted) she emitted an easy sigh.

'Ah, at last, nature,' she said. Yet she was coming from the jungle . . .

The trouble is that the equatorial jungle, on both the right and left of the river, makes a terrible racket.

---

* Though I stayed in Para three weeks I must have got them lost somewhere in my life.

Para, Para . . . nothing appears.

† The Amazon is often twenty miles wide, but the islands block the view.

Ah! I'm here, feeling tiny and neglected, in the back of
 this ship; which, too, is a huge voyage of hundreds
 and hundreds of days, the first was such a long
 while ago, then others, gone, gone, all these hundreds, and now then this last one and finally
 Europe, and in Europe there's By,*

By, quick, pay attention,
I'm back, By, it's me, hi!

Pretty miss, my darling!
Pretty miss, my darling!

How cold the air is tonight.

In Europe is Paris.
Paris, big brothel where French is spoken.
I'm counting on you to get this finished.
Paris . . .
Paris? and what then?
Boy, this homecoming has its cramps!

At last the North Wind.
No more tropical breezes.
This North one hates me, martyrs me.
Admits it.
But the one over there—the tropical—who's playing
                                                absent
Satisfies every bit of you
But ever so sweetly drains you,
Sucks you dry,
And when you wake months later . . . finished . . .

* A woman's name. [Translator's note]

I've done a Narcissus of my own.
But for quite a while my diary has been annoying me.
I'm returning without an overcoat.
That also annoys me.
With an earache and no idea what to do and that too
annoys me.
And She, She, By, what can she have done with her
whole year?
It strikes me that I have done my share of whining on
this trip.
It was stronger than I—a kind of debt toward my
childhood. I know me.
It's nice to think I could go through with it
(Better known as a rebellious, bad-tempered sad-sack).
In Lisbon this morning I read the *Times*.
(Boy, is it stupid!)
And some new books.
Good as gold these rebels in France; adorable writers;
pretty despairing ladies
One's just seen your despair at the movies.
It's always so graceful.

three days later

Hey, still shaking?
Why, of course, we're to arrive tomorrow.
France, France, and he's all
Upset because he's coming home.

a bit later

He talks loud, he is rude,
He is fat, he spews joy.
So he hasn't changed.

A victim as much of good events as of bad.
In a word impressed.
Let's get it finished.

15th. Evening debarkation at Le Havre

PREFACE TO SOME RECOLLECTIONS

Seeing a huge year reduced to so few pages the author is astonished. Surely there must have been lots of other things.

So he rummages around. Nothing. Or, if not nothing, mists.

Finally to mask his embarrassment he assumes a professorial voice.

H. M.

THE INDIAN'S CABIN IN THE CORDILLERA OF THE ANDES

The Indian's cabin is not any modest chalet. No, it is something absolutely revolting. But its intimacy is such that after a few months in one you cannot imagine yourself living anywhere else.

To the white man the Indian's cabin is just one more proof of his idiocy. And it is true of course that it does not have a chimney. And quite a number of other items are also lacking. But *not having* one thing of necessity means *having* something else. Which is why the Indian's cabin yields such a definite plus. It is crammed full. You enter, threading your way through all kinds of thickness. It exudes darkness, a well-padded, smoke-crammed darkness . . . No chimney, just smoke. The white man's habitations have no center. They have windows.

The Indian's cabin is just that—nothing, nothing from without, all from within. That smoke is from the corn they are roasting for dinner. The smoke both chokes and caresses you, then goes slowly out the door to make room for more smoke, warmer, more recently left the wood.

Crammed full of anesthesia, of smells, of filth, of people.

Just full.

The Salvation Army apparently is considering dispatching over there some dedicated idiots, who will teach the Indians how to pierce their chimneys. But then what will the Indian have left? He needs his wealth.

One more thing is to know the earth from the bottom up, to hold it respectfully by the feet and know it in its whole stretched-out length. And you have to know it stretched out.

His cabin is also a place marvelously suited for playing music. They pipe into a kind of Pan's flute, delighting in a much reiterated phrase which tells more about themselves than any one other thing they do or work at, their pot-making included. Here is how it goes. At the beginning a three-note group, the first of which is not very high (the Arabs start much higher, carried away), the second higher, and the third down again—and exactly as much down as the previous one has been up (interval often of a third). Then another three-note group, for which the first is again the pivot, the second up, and the last down; then other groups of three with here and there an occasional, insignificant trill. And the whole, after several attempts to attain an elevation (which constitutes the range of the phrase), falls back, settling to that bottom note which is its end, or rather its suicide, or even better its mortal exhaustion. That open water where it had to founder.

ALCOHOL

The Indian enjoys getting drunk like nobody else, and the smoke in his cabin is but the necessary small change. He has the reputation of being a brute. Possibly. But when it comes to drinking he knows what he is up to.

First, don't get drunk one evening or two. No, they get drunk for three weeks straight—beginning, say, with the feast of San Juan—not letting up for an instant and their wives pouring it into their mouths once they are no longer completely blacked out. They are not looking for separate little emotions, like getting high, or more coordinated, none of that jumble of bits and pieces which the White Man likes. No. He concentrates himself and from this center assaults the drink—eyeing it, pushing it, jostling it, mauling it—with a courage, a coolness, an impassivity, and, most of all, a singleness of purpose that takes your breath away.

He has made up his mind to have alcohol. O.K., so he really gives himself the works. For days you will not see him even stumble, then toward the sixth or seventh he will all of a sudden fall down, arms crossed. I have seen a whole settlement like this—out with their arms crossed—they got my horse frightened.

There were some people still reeling about in their ponchos, but this was rarer. There were also some corpses.

Of any drug they ask the same thing, and since they know how to wait it all ends by giving them the same thing. They don't give a damn about the preliminaries, they want the intoxication to engulf them and knock them out, they want to be defeated.

TATTOO MARKS

The jungle Indians do not, in the strict sense, tattoo themselves. That is, they do not make deep incisions in their skins.

They may make a design on their faces to go have lunch at a friend's, then rub it out on the way home. Everyone has mentioned how attractive this is. There are certain colors, however, that smudge badly. For us they would be an inconvenience. The Turks were quite right to have pointed out how unseemly a face is. There it is on top of your clothing, sticking out, with glances escaping from it like madmen. Everything unhealthy and bestial that your skin has about it vanishes with the application of a line, a spot of rouge. Your face becomes not so much intelligent as intellectual, it becomes *witty*. That calms. It was always my feeling when my Indians had tattooed themselves that now we would be able to talk (the exception being the case where the design confines itself to a stupid exaggeration of the facial contours and their one or two basic elements).

It does not take much of a prophet to predict that before long the white race will on its own take up tattooing. I am told that current opinion is flatly opposed to this—and much else. Prophets say, 'You'll see'; that suffices for both them and me.

I only add that tattooing, like all ornamentation, can both bring out a surface and even more readily make the same surface disappear, just as a tapestry makes the whole length of a wall disappear. Well, now is the time to have the face disappear. It is truly impossible with a face to have a modest look—provided that it has not been specially arranged for that.

PIROGUES

'A long hollow that preserves you from the waters,' as this explorer said. Now a second long hollow is put over you—this one made out of leaves and sticks—all of it absolutely watertight and preserving you not only from rain and sun but also from any view of the water or sky, right and left banks, the aft, or your helmsman up there on the deck, from any view except the strictly frontal, and from all communications, either pedestrian or oral. (And the view ahead is no more than a mere opening, not very big, and almost round.) You would think you were in a telescope. It is called a *pamakari*. The combination of frequent downpours and very strong sun renders it indispensable.

A tunnel, yes, low, stifling. A tunnel walled up in back, with but one exit, gradually sloping down until it reaches a point two-thirds of the way along the total boat deck, which it hermetically seals. You commit yourself to one of these impasses as to some huge gullet. And pirogues with *pamakaris* have that look of a gullet which is about to close. You live down there eighteen hours a day, lying, not moving, just lying there, prone, you have to be lying since it is not high enough for you to sit up. Imprisoned there, not knowing what is going on, you either work yourself into a rage or you doze off. This is what from afar Europeans take for the picture of freedom.

THE ANDEAN CORDILLERA

Look at what the earth's fate has been—to have had each bit of her either shunted into something else, or else replanted. In Europe more and more keeps disappearing. And who has done this? We, men and plants. So that now there is nothing left for her to be at all proud about. This is why it is so breath-taking to have set in front of you, at a height of 13,000 feet, this spectacle of protestation going across South America; this enormous hunk of earth that is the Andean chain and which goes from the north to the south of this long semicontinent without once weakening, and with a breadth perfectly in keeping. It has nothing to show you but earth, and would not think of apologizing for having but that.

'But come on, is that all that there is?'

'Of course, earth, earth, earth.'

At the beginning you are apt to feel queasy; because while man can do without animals, he does need some plant life. Vegetables have a certain juice that he likes—and the color green.

How different the ocean's fate has been. The whole world, to be sure, has gone over it. The Phoenicians, the Chinese, the Romans in their galleys, the *Mauretania* but an hour ago. Yes, but there is no record. This is one whore who is always a virgin.

In monotony itself there is a somewhat misunderstood virtue, for the reason that the repetition of any one object is worth no matter what variety of objects. It has its own very special importance, due partly to the fact that you can only barely state it in writing, and not at all in a visual form. A tree, for instance, is much more easily described than a forest. The difficulty comes in having to describe so many different trees. The concentration of attention and time each requires is so vast that compared to everything else that claims us they are not worth it—worth the extra year it would take to examine a forest. It nonetheless impresses us, if only because it has remained above our efforts to describe it.

What country would make on you more of an impression than one planted in nothing but street lights? Street lights, identical street lights to infinity. Think of Germany from one end to another covered with just beer barrels! To imagine devices still more sophisticated seems a little pointless.

If a man of foresight were to propose doing something new for the eye with a dab of water, you would hardly expect his associates (supposing there were any) not to laugh at him. What is more nil, more inconsistent than a dab of water? Still it is with this that he would have formed the ocean. An ocean is simply the recurrence of a dab of water, a sizable recurrence . . .

And there is nothing on this planet that has such a hold on you as the sea. To the sea you devote yourself as to a religion. Where is the Swiss girl who can claim as much?

By the same token the simplest, most monotonous existence must also be the most attractive.

The hermit regaining his cabin for the fifty thousandth time must feel something extraordinary. Imagine the significance to him of a cabin present fifty thousand times within him, and which for all that remains both *external* and *single* and . . . there.

In holding to a set way of acting lies possibly the only real greatness.

It is superfluous to point out how many travelers lose, in setting their thoughts to paper, any claim to greatness (causes and effects are a little mixed here), or why this should be so common among the species of philosopher ignorant of life. Some of them are so taken up by this obsession with recurrence that they have ended by seeing no more than the *being* in each being, a point to which they have arrived in perfectly good faith. The fellow's wife, a dog, an owl, a willow: being, being, being. He sees their difference, but the notion of something recurring intoxicates him beyond any question of differentiation.

HOSPITALITY

Ecuador is one of those countries you can even now cross without any other money than the title of caballero. The Ecuadorian is not simply hospitable in an unheard-of style. He actually enjoys giving.

On a boat the Ecuadorian will treat the whole ship to a drink. And it hurts him very much not to be able to invite by radio all the ships going in his direction to draw up alongside.

I have had pointed out to me more than one ruined ex-multi-millionaire who had got himself that way just through giving. One particularly struck me. He was modest, well-mannered, self-effacing—a really passionless man. He had been worth some six million sucres (one sucre=one dollar), and when he saw anyone he had to give him something. A horse? A carpet? A piano? A ring? If you did not immediately answer, 'No thank you,' he would say, 'Ah, I really knew you would like this,' and from then on not even your slap would have got him to go back on his decision. If you were absent-minded or alert enough to say aloud that such and such a thing was rather nice, he would answer that it was yours. No one ever left his home in quite the same shape as he had entered it. And if you saw in the street a couple of porters, or some wheelbarrows being directed by someone, it was customary to say that he was on his way home from M.D.'s.

There are some saints who have made a specialty of giving. For them religion was that. The man who gives forms for himself, as he goes on, a more and more massive idea of what happiness is.

If you give a possession of yours—and it can be something quite neutral, nominally worthless—to someone else who actually needs it, *its value* is returned in the look of happiness that you see.

Thus whatever you own has a potential happiness value. All you need do is find the pauper, the child, the person for whom this holds. To be able to amass whole spectacles of happiness! To be a happiness factory. The urge is so strong that several people have become beggars in order to have something to give. The solution is to be sure not the most straightforward, but people have such a real need for signs that a happy man without an external sign of happiness would by just this be quite unhappy.

The joy of giving is not always, as generally believed, pure kindness. There was at the Para zoo (Brazil) a worker whom all the animals adored. He would offer them food. One chimpanzee used to jump to the ground the moment he heard him whistle, no matter how far away he might be (a savage one at that, ornery, never looking out unless he felt like it, and that probably not five times a day).

The man would come by, and the chimpanzee would grab hold of his head in hands that could just as easily have torn it off. Only instead he would very delicately support it against his bars and kiss it some, a good while, then brusquely go off to squat on a crate and not move another muscle. And he would not take the food which the man occasionally offered him (occasionally, for he was regular in nothing) until long after he had gone away.

This scene, perhaps because of what I cannot manage to say, or even think, about it, moved me very much. When this workman saw how moved I was, he said to me, 'I used to go there every day, that's why he was more friendly. I spend my real time giving the alligators whacks across the eyes with my cane.' Another time he said, 'Animals are things I can't stand, they take everything too seriously.' He was giving, therefore, without reaching the point of being impressed by the sight of the happiness he had brought about. Also he may not have been giving enough. Or perhaps he just had not gotten underway. There was something fishy, mean guy, about him. It may also be that he had that lover's feeling of being clung to. He must have felt tied down. As for the chimpanzee it was plain that he would die of grief if he were not to see him again. Even now I am not sure that I have been able to express it well enough, but the understanding between this chimpanzee and this man was quite out of the ordinary, unique . . . and, what's more, this man had something nasty about him . . .